REACH *Beyond* *Your Grasp*

Embracing Dreams That Reflect God's Best for You — *And* Achieving Them

M. Blaine Smith

SilverCrest
B•O•O•K•S

SilverCrest Books
P.O. Box 448
Damascus, Maryland 20872

e-mail: scr@nehemiahministries.com
www.nehemiahministries.com

Library of Congress Control Number: 2012906696

ISBN: 978-0-9840322-5-9

I

The Courage
to Dream

1

Dare to Dream

*It is extraordinarily important to give myself the
freedom to dream big, and to view my dreams with
an optimistic bias.*

WHAT IF???

What if, five years from now, say, you could be in the job of
your dreams? A job that draws marvelously on your gifts, gives
you liberal control over what you accomplish and ample opportunity to make a meaningful contribution to life. Any idea what it
would be?

What if, during this same period—or sooner—you could accomplish cherished dreams in other areas where you have potential? Is there an athletic, musical, artistic or creative talent you'd
like to develop? An achievement you'd like to realize? A degree
you'd like to earn?

What about your personal ministry and mission? Is there a spiritual gift you'd like to nurture? A program or project you'd like to
launch? An area of service to others where you'd like to become
active and proficient?

And what about the world of friendships, relationships and family life? Do you long for more friendships or deeper ones? If you're single, do you cherish the hope for marriage? If you're married, do you wish for children? Are there goals for your marriage relationship or family life you'd like to achieve?

Do you dream of improving your lifestyle in certain ways? Long for a better home? Wish to live in a different part of this country or in another one? Desire certain benefits that would make life more comfortable or enable you to better realize your potential? Hope for a blessed retirement?

What about the vital matter of your spiritual life? Do you long for a deeper relationship with Christ? Greater confidence of his guidance? A more thankful spirit? Success in conquering a habit that's hindering God's best for you?

If you are able to give a clear and passionate answer to any of these questions, then this book is intended for you. I'll do my best to help you determine which dreams are truly best for you, and to encourage you to embrace them wholeheartedly. I'll also offer as much practical advice as I can about how to pursue them and achieve them. This is a book about how to dream, and how to do so successfully.

Nothing Lights My Fire

Perhaps you're not able to give a confident answer to any of these questions. You may identify with a woman who confessed to me recently in sad sincerity, "I don't desire anything." You might not go this far; still, you'll admit that no major dreams are driving your life right now, perhaps not for a long time. If so, this book is still meant for you, and I urge you to read it with an open heart. By becoming—may I say it?—a more effective dreamer about your life and destiny, you can improve the quality of your life greatly, as well as its benefit to others.

Of this much I'm certain: you've *had* dreams, and you've had big ones. If you dig back far enough, you'll find a time when you experienced intense hope for your future and dreams that stirred you deeply. Over time they lost their force—through discouragement, setbacks, too much criticism, perhaps. Yet your capacity to dream is still strong. And dreams that have long been repressed will easily resurface, given the right encouragement.

My sincerest hope is that this book will help you to reclaim these dreams, as well as to lock in to new ones that are right for you. May I ask you at least to lay hold to one dream as you begin this book? Envision yourself experiencing greater motivation, and aspirations that bring greater energy and purpose to all you do. Focus on that image, and enjoy it. Hope for it as fully as you can. That is a most worthy goal for investing time with this or any book, and may it be rewarded as you read!

But, I'm a Christian, and . . .

Perhaps, though, your response was more like this: *As a Christian, I'm simply confused about how to respond to my dreams. Of course I have them; in fact, I have intense desires for my future. I'd love to know God wants me to take them seriously. But it's terribly hard to believe that he does. Scripture reminds us so often that our desires are untrustworthy and evil, and urges us to deny them.*

And what about my responsibility to lay down my life for the sake of others? As a Christian, I'm called to sacrifice myself for others' needs, right? I'm to look for the most glaring needs in the world and do what I can to help with them. Of course dreams I might have to serve others or to deepen my relationship with Christ have value. But I don't see how my more personal dreams can possibly benefit Christ's mission.

If your response was anywhere along these lines, then this book is *especially* intended for you. My primary concern is to help Christians learn what it is to dream in a manner that's healthy and Christ-honoring. I assure you at the outset that this *doesn't* mean putting dreams related to your needs and personal potential on the back burner. I understand profoundly the issues we Christians struggle with in confronting such dreams, and the torturous guilt we can experience even in just considering them. I've been there often, as have many I've known and counseled.

Yet over forty-six years of walking with Christ, I've only grown more convinced that having dreams based on the gifts and interests most central to our personality, and strong dedication to following them, not only honors Christ, but is essential to living our life in way that most fully benefits others.

Yes, we can buy in to dreams that have nothing to do with God's best for our life, and that lead us down the primrose path. No approach to finding God's will is risk-free. But there is a radically positive side to the equation. God also uses our dreams, and those desires that are strongest and most consistent within us, to move us in directions that are uniquely right for our life, and that best position us to be a channel of his grace to the world.

Throughout this book, I'll look at many of the issues that are unique to us as Christians in embracing personal dreams. I'll draw as fully as I can on Scripture, and show how the Bible, when clearly understood, encourages us to dream big about our future and to pursue important dreams passionately. I'll look also at misleading notions and interpretations of Scripture that discourage us from following our aspirations.

Most important, I want to encourage you as a Christian to think big about your life—to lock in to those dreams that are most important in God's plan for you, and to move toward them with courageous optimism.

When We're Heading

The good news is that you *can* learn to think with grander vision about your life and to follow that vision with greater confidence. To that end, we'll look at four broad areas related to realizing personal dreams.

• **Follow your passions.** *Why we should feel comfortable as Christians embracing dreams in a wide variety of areas, and optimistic about our possibilities for success.* I'll consider what this optimism entails, why it's essential to our Christian walk, and why it's important that we "follow our bliss."

• **Establishing the right dreams.** *Identifying, from the multitude of options, those dreams that are most appropriate for us personally and most reflective of God's intentions for our life.* What weight should we give to our personal desires vs. the needs of others in determining our life's mission? What if a dream no longer fits our life as we now know it, even though we were strongly inspired to follow it in the past? How do we know if God has closed the door on a dream, or if our limitations rule it out? These are all concerns we'll explore.

• **Getting your life in motion toward a dream.** *Determining a plan of action, breaking the inertia and establishing momentum.* I'll discuss how to set goals effectively and take the first steps toward a dream. I'll also give advice for seeking help when you need it, and for praying effectively about your dreams and goals.

I'll also offer perspective for staying hopeful and persistent for the period required to reach a dream. We're usually too quick to think that setbacks indicate God is nixing a dream. In fact, they are often surmountable. And we often find that circumstances appearing negative do bring us remarkable benefit in time. I'll provide guidelines for evaluating setbacks and for viewing them as optimistically as possible.

• **Reaping the harvest.** *Learning to succeed joyfully, and to keep our desire for new adventure strong once we've achieved a dream.* We sometimes sabotage a dream that is well within our reach. Or we may achieve it but fail to enjoy our victory as fully as we should. At the other extreme, success can soften us, and dampen our zeal to embrace new dreams. I'll consider these challenges in the final section. I'll offer counsel for overcoming fears of success, and for staying in a growth mode after we've reached important horizons.

My concern throughout this book is to help you as a Christian accomplish three broad objectives:

• to identify and embrace those dreams that are most important
for your life personally
    • to find the courage to pursue them and to persevere until you
achieve them
    • to develop healthy biblical thinking on these matters, and to
work through issues that stand in the way of taking your personal
dreams seriously.

Positive Thinking for the Thinking Christian
If I may boil it down to *one* objective, it's to help you view your life
and your future with the eyes of faith. I want to encourage faith-
inspired thinking that stimulates you to realize your potential and
become all that Christ has created you to be.

Our single greatest need as Christians is to achieve an outlook
of faith. All of the great promises of Scripture, while assured to us
as gifts of God's grace, are to be received on our part by faith. "For
it is by grace you have been saved, *through faith . . .*" (Eph 2:8
emphasis added).

This faith, as Scripture understands it, is an extraordinarily optimistic perception of God and his intentions for our life. We
shouldn't underestimate what this optimism ought to mean in terms
of how we view our possibilities and, especially, those dreams that
most ignite us. Our beginning assumption should be that God wants
us to take them seriously. We should assume that as we pursue them,
he'll open doors and make it possible for us to accomplish them. If
success isn't possible, we'll still be better off for having tried, and
others will benefit greatly as well. We should assume, too, that when
we experience setbacks, they have silver linings, and in time may
even prove to be open doors in disguise.

To say it as strongly as possible, we're called to an optimistic
bias as we pursue our dreams. When we have reason to believe a
dream respects the gifts and interests God has given us, we should
move toward it with the conviction we'll succeed. This belief is
critically important, for it enhances our success in numerous ways.

There are many perspectives of faith that make up this optimistic bias and contribute to keeping it healthy and strong, and we'll explore some of the most important in the pages ahead. It helps us greatly in internalizing these perspectives to identify them precisely and to express them as succinctly as we can. To help with this process, I've summarized the key point of each chapter in a sentence or two, which I call a "Faith Expectation." I note these Faith Expectations at the beginning of each chapter, and express them in the first person—to encourage you to adopt them as personal statements of faith.

I urge you to read the Faith Expectation before beginning a chapter and to take a moment to reflect on it. After finishing the chapter, come back and consider the Faith Expectation again more carefully and how it applies to the realities of your life. You may find it helpful to keep a journal of thoughts and resolutions that occur while you're reading.

I encourage you also to review these Faith Expectations often, especially those that challenge pessimistic outlooks that are typical for you.

Mining the Field Ahead

Please note also that while the chapters are consecutive and unfold in obvious ways, I've written each one as an inspirational piece in itself. As with most books, you'll derive an important benefit from reading the chapters in order. Yet if you find that certain ones relate more obviously to your needs, there's no harm reading them first. This book is given to strengthen your faith, and each chapter makes its own special contribution. Draw on this book in whatever way most helps you.

One earnest request: Read this book itself with an optimistic bias—that God has far greater possibilities for your life than you've even begun to imagine. Stay open and expectant as you read. Expect God to clarify new directions for you—perhaps even radical changes you should make.

Stay *inquisitive* as you read. Constantly ask questions—of yourself, of life and of God. Consider what are your deepest aspirations, where your greatest potential lies, and how you can best invest it to meet the needs of a desperately hurting world. Consider with brutal honesty what you would do with your life if finances were not an issue and fear not an obstacle. Simply asking the right questions helps beyond words.

Often one simple question will suffice.

What if?

2

Passion and Availability

*My passion for a dream, and my availability to pursue it,
put me in a significant position of strength as I begin
moving toward it.*

WHEN MY FATHER WAS A HIGH SCHOOL JUNIOR, he locked
in to a dream: he would become the world's champion endurance
bicyclist.

An audacious aspiration for a frail sixteen-year-old with no previous athletic achievements to his credit, we might say.

Not as it turned out.

It was 1927, and, establishing endurance records had become a
national craze in the optimistic mania of this pre-depression period. A friend of Dad's, Owen Evens, had set one in golf—playing
17 hours without a break. A Frenchman held the record for non-
stop cycling, at 24 hours. The Amateur Bicycle League was urging
American cyclists to try to top it.

Dad had taken a job as a bicycle messenger that summer. He
found his stamina held up well, even after hours of peddling furiously around Washington streets in sweltering heat. One day he

made a simple connection between his experience as a messenger and winning the endurance title. "I can do it," he thought. "I can beat that Frenchman's record."

On August 17, at 9:00 p.m., he officially began his quest for the title, peddling a circular path around the polo grounds of Washington, D.C.'s Hain's Point. Officials from the Amateur Bicycle League were on hand to monitor his progress, and members of the local press as well.

When he finally eased his brakeless, gearless bike to a stop and stumbled off, it was 9:27 p.m.—August 18. He had stayed aloft for 24 hours and 27 minutes, peddling 250 miles and setting a new world record.

Local papers featured many articles about the event—announcing Dad's intention to try for the title, detailing his marathon ride while in progress, then reporting his victory and follow-up news. The titles of these now barely readable, yellowed clippings, pasted in an ancient, ragged scrapbook, still give me chills to read:

"Youth Will Try for Endurance Record on Bike"
"Smith Sure He Will Break Bicycle Record"
"Milton Smith, Washington Marathon Cycler, Grinds Along"
"Marathon Cyclist Going Strong after 12 Hours"
"Bike Rider Nearing Record in Grind at Potomac Park"
"Marathon Cyclist Sets New Endurance Record"
"Record Is Claimed by Capital Bikeman"
"Local Youth Claims New Bicycle Record"
"District Boy Sets Bike Record: Milton Smith Rides 250.4 Miles
    in 24-¼ Hours"
"Courage Helped Smith in Bike Grind"
"Smith, D.C. Bikeman, after World Mark"

United Press also picked up the story in a feature carried by many papers around the country. The result of all this media attention was that Dad became an overnight celebrity in Washington. A shy, barely-known Eastern High School student gained a cherished new identity. Achieving his goal boosted his confidence immensely, and gave him the heart to think big as he moved into college and adulthood. The benefits to every area of his life were enormous.

Dreams That Work

Two things impress me about my dad's successful pursuit of the endurance title. For one, I'm moved by the fact that he took his dream to win it so seriously. He wanted this prize so badly that he found the resolve and means to attain it.

When we look honestly at why some dreams of ours succeed while others fail, we usually find that only the strong ones survive. It's fundamental to our nature as humans to have aspirations, and over a lifetime we experience many. It's just as basic to our nature to lose heart; it takes practically nothing to discourage us and convince us that a dream is impossible for us. Yet when a dream is substantial enough, and our passion to achieve it strong enough, we find a way to beat the challenges and persevere till we succeed. It also seems that serendipities occur: life rises up to meet us and help us accomplish what we desire.

The older I grow, the more impressed I am with what a gift it is to experience a dream at this level. When we see a real-life example of someone who benefited from a dream this powerful, it's always inspiring.

Of course, by today's standards my father's accomplishment, while impressive, doesn't seem that earth-shattering. Cyclists have established and broken countless endurance records in the 85 years since dad made his marathon sojourn around that Washington park. What all this history suggests is that there were undoubtedly many— probably thousands—in the United States at that time who could have achieved this same feat. Yet among those who could have done so with a reasonable try, only my father made the effort at that time. The fact that he tried made the difference.

This same dynamic operates far more frequently in our experience than most of us realize. We often hold back from pursuing a dream because we fear "the competition." We assume so many others are vying for the same benefit that we have no hope of attaining it. Yet when we begin moving earnestly toward a goal, we're sometimes surprised: we find that far fewer have found the heart to try for it than we supposed. The mere fact that we've made ourselves available for the opportunity puts us in a position of strength, and makes it possible for us to succeed.

Our personal dreams so frequently *are* within our reach. My dad's experience is one small example of how passion and availability can tip the scales.

A Lifetime Need

It's hard to exaggerate the importance of personal dreams. The benefits they bring to our well-being, health, productivity, social life and personal growth defy description. If we look carefully at our life, we always find that the times when we've felt most alive and most hopeful about our future, have been when we've embraced a dream and pursued it eagerly. These also have been the times when our life has been most fruitful and beneficial to others.

We need dreams like the air we breathe. We need them in career, education, relationships, avocations, lifestyle, personal development and growth. And we need fresh dreams throughout our life: when one is realized, it's important to replace it with another, that we remain forever in a growth mode. Major dreams may be realized even at unlikely points late in life. Consider Henry J. Magaziner, who published his first book at 89—a coffee-table volume on classic iron works that received critical acclaim. Magaziner didn't begin this project till he was 81.[1]

Yet for a dream to be effective—to the point it propels us to succeed—we must own it so fully that it becomes part of the fabric of our personality. This won't happen unless we're convinced our dreams are both important and achievable.

David's Exuberance for Life

We find inspiration to both of these ends in the story of David and

Goliath. I've often drawn on this incident in my *Nehemiah Notes* articles, for it has much to teach us about realizing our potential. Yet for a long time I missed a critical detail about David's decision to fight the giant that stunned me once I noticed it.

When Goliath taunted the army of Israel, demanding that a warrior come forth and fight him, Saul offered a reward to any citizen able to meet the challenge. David heard soldiers talking about this prize while he was visiting his brothers on the front line: "Do you see how this man keeps coming out? He comes out to defy Israel. The king will give great wealth to the man who kills him. He will also give him his daughter in marriage and will exempt his father's family from taxes in Israel" (1 Sam 17:25).

After hearing this tantalizing description of Saul's reward, David asked two further groups of soldiers for information about it, "and the men answered him as before" (v. 30).

What impressed me when I finally noticed it, after years of teaching and writing on this passage, is that this reward *influenced* David's decision to fight Goliath. And substantially. This is clear from the level of interest David showed in confirming the details about it.

The reward promised several benefits to the victorious warrior: a marriage partner, financial security, political freedom, and—by implication—the chance to exercise leadership and political influence. David obviously had dreams in some or all of these areas, and saw fighting Goliath as an opportunity to take a quantum leap toward them. And his motivation in these areas was undoubtedly stronger than that of most of his contemporaries, for he alone mustered the courage to confront the giant.

David, to be sure, also possessed strong faith in God, and ached to see God's glory defended against Goliath's slander (1 Sam 17:26, 36, 45-47). He clearly felt strong compassion for his countrymen too, and longed to help free them from the Philistines' oppression. These were substantial dreams in themselves.

Yet we shouldn't downplay the role that David's hope for certain personal benefits played in deciding to accept Goliath's wager.

What this story reveals most importantly is that David had *a passion for life*. It was reflected in several major longings: to improve his own life in certain ways, to help his countrymen, and to uphold God's glory. *All* of these desires were important in his gaining the motivation to fight Goliath. And it was precisely because they were so strong that he found the strength of heart to do something this supremely challenging.

David's example is so refreshing, for it encourages us both to take our personal dreams seriously and to allow them to become powerful inspirations. Many Christians are uncomfortable giving much attention to their dreams—especially those for personal benefits—out of fear their aspirations might interfere with their devotion to Christ. Our dreams can become idols, unquestionably. Yet C. S. Lewis nailed this problem when he noted that we fail, not by loving things too much, but by not loving God enough. If I'm attaching too much importance to an otherwise healthy dream, the answer isn't to try to tone down my enthusiasm for it, but to strive to increase my affection for Christ.

It's here that David's role model is so helpful. Because his devotion to God was so strong, his personal aspirations influenced him in a healthy manner. His example inspires us both to strengthen our relationship with Christ *and* to embrace substantial dreams for our life. David's experience also suggests that within the context of a strong relationship with God, we'll be inclined to live out our dreams in ways that most help others and enhance Christ's mission.

By the same token, we see in David's countrymen the problem that occurs when personal dreams are not strong enough. It's fair to say that if some of them had possessed a stronger passion for life, they, like David, would have been clamoring to fight the giant.

The Availability Factor
Which brings us to another lesson David's experience with Goliath teaches. It's the fact that others may *not* be clamoring to accom-

plish the same dreams we want to pursue.

The lack of competition David faced in fighting Goliath was beyond any belief. His conviction that he could tackle the giant sprang from recalling successes as a shepherd fighting wild animals with a sling (I Sam 17:34-37). Since God's glory was now at stake, David assumed God would give victory through this skill already so evident in his life. Yet thousands of Israelite soldiers had also been shepherds or hunters and had confronted ravenous animals just as David did. They had the identical basis for concluding they could successfully battle Goliath. But none of them made this connection. *Not one.* David alone was able to see the situation with the eyes of faith.

Why did David see a remarkable opportunity for victory, while others didn't? His passion for life explains it, I'm sure. It was so strong that he was motivated to make connections between his past experience and the present challenge that others didn't bother to try to make.

The failure of other Israelites to see this situation optimistically also demonstrates how inherently human it is to expect failure, even when the prospect for success is excellent. Regardless how achievable a dream may be, others simply may not believe it's possible for them. While it's tragic that people often fail to recognize golden opportunities, it's a reason for encouragement whenever we fear others may crowd us out of reaching a desired goal. We may find, as my dad did in the endurance contest, that the competition is insignificant. And our availability alone may make our success possible, if we just make a reasonable effort. No story in Scripture illustrates this dynamic better than that of David and Goliath.

Follow Your Star

David's encounter with Goliath, then, helps us to think in terms of doors being open rather than closed. And his passion for life, which this incident reveals so vividly, inspires us to take our own dreams seriously. We're encouraged both to dream big and to embrace our dreams with greater confidence. Remember David's experience with Goliath whenever you're entertaining a major step with your life.

Perhaps you'll find it helpful, too, to remember Milton Smith cycling endless circles around Hain's Point in August 1927, and persisting till he achieved his goal. His experience inspires me for obvious reasons—because of my relation to him, and because the event is part of our family history. Yet you may find inspiration in it as well because of the timeless lesson it offers—that passion and availability greatly enhance our potential for accomplishing a dream.

Keep both these points strongly in mind as you weigh possibilities for your future. If there's a dream you earnestly want to pursue, see yourself in a position of strength simply because you desire it so much. And see your willingness to follow it as a position of strength also. If competition is an issue, others will probably not find this same resolve to take on this dream. And getting your life moving toward it will cause the dynamics to work in your favor in many ways.

I have much more to say about getting that dream in motion in the pages ahead, so please continue to read. And I have lots of encouragement to offer for staying in motion as long as it takes to reach your goal. Here, again, I hope my father's image in that cycling contest is helpful—for riding out a dream to the finish makes all the difference.

3

Your Life's Bigger Picture

My limitations, no matter how severe, will not prevent me from reaching a dream God intends me to achieve. I should give far more attention to my gifts and aspirations than to my limitations, in considering God's direction for my life.

"HOW CAN I TAKE ALL YOUR MONEY, and leave you broke and penniless?"

Greg Lukens welcomed me to his warehouse with his standard greeting. I liked him the moment I met him, and was impressed with his style. He knew I'd be spending more than pocket change there, and he'd defused my anxiety about doing so.

I was equally impressed as I watched him navigate the cavernous facility that is Washington Professional Sound. The company occupies a vast subterranean world beneath the street shops of Grandview Avenue, in Wheaton, Maryland—the confines of a former bowling alley. Greg knows every cubic centimeter of this vastly-stocked outlet—the location of hundreds of specialty products, stacked to the ceiling on narrow rows of metal shelves, and their minute specifications. He knows his 40 employees by name and can recognize them by voice.

Washington Professional Sound sells high-end audio products to the highest-end customers. It's the place a major recording studio will contact to purchase a 24-track analog tape recorder, or one of those endless mixing boards you see pictured on the cover of audio magazines, with 600 knobs. It's where a radio station will turn to order a special broadcast microphone more expensive than a diamond necklace.

I was there to purchase some recording equipment for my ministry, costing around $2,000, making me, I'm sure, Greg's low-end customer of the week. Yet he treated me with respect, and gave me careful instructions about how to operate the items I'd selected.

If you had accompanied me that day on my visit to Washington Professional Sound, you might not have noticed anything unusual about Greg Lukens' world until you entered his office. It was only then that the stark reality of his situation struck me fully. I watched in astonishment as Greg sat down at his desk to type out an invoice on his computer—one consisting of a keyboard, tower, speakers . . . but no monitor. At first I was stunned by this bizarre omission. It quickly soaked through my leaden skull that a monitor wouldn't benefit Greg a bit, for he couldn't see one pixel on it. Greg, you see, is blind. Not just "legally blind," but *totally* blind—the result of a tragic spill off a dirt bike when he was sixteen years old.

In spite of this considerable handicap, he not only founded this multi-million-dollar business, but manages its day-to-day operations.

And types comfortably on his personal computer. He has it jury-rigged to "speak" to him—to announce each letter he types, and to beep at him rudely after each typo.

It was a wake-up call like few I've experienced in a long time. As I drove home, I thought of the many problems I bemoan in my own life that are very minor limitations next to Greg's blindness. I felt like God was shaking me by the shoulders, saying, "Stop dwelling on your disadvantages. Stop worrying about what you don't have. Focus on what you *do* have—the resources, gifts and opportunities I've given you—and give your energy to making the best of them."

Not Dwelling on Our Limitations

We hardly face a greater challenge in life than knowing how to weigh our personal limitations. Each of us, as we look at our life, is aware—often profoundly conscious—of certain limitations we have. These may include, as in Greg's case, an actual physical disability. More typically they involve limits in our talent or potential in areas we regard as important, shortcomings in our physical appearance, deficiencies in our health, less overall energy than we'd like to have, and circumstances we believe are stacked against us. And, of course, there's our finances. Which one of us ever feels we have all the money we need to achieve our goals?

Against these limitations we have dreams—those things we would like to accomplish with our life. It can be extremely difficult to know what weight we should give to our limitations in considering whether or not to pursue a dream. Should we regard them as an absolute barrier to our achieving the dream—perhaps even a sign from God that we shouldn't move ahead? Or should we believe, in faith, that God will give us success in spite of them?

Greg Lukens' example is one of those remarkable ones we encounter from time to time, which suggest that we ought to tilt more toward the latter perspective than the former. We need examples like Greg's to inspire us, for frankly the tendency for many of us—even when a dream fits our potential well—is to cave in too easily to our limitations. We assume they're a roadblock to our ever being successful. Yet Greg's example reminds us that even the most serious limitation may not be an obstacle to our succeeding, so much as a problem we can learn to overcome.

Focusing on Our Advantages

When I consider the factors that have contributed to Greg's success, at the top of the list is the fact that he is by nature a problem solver. This is evident as soon as you meet him. The whole bent of his personality is toward finding ways to make things work.

We each will do well to look carefully at how we use our own mental energy most of the time. Even those of us who are most intelligent may not focus our thinking in a way that is constructive, or that opens us to God's best for our life. Many highly intelligent people use their brilliance far more to try to justify to themselves why their dreams cannot be realized, than to look for ways to achieve them. When this is the thrust of our thinking, we almost surely doom ourselves to failure.

The fact is that we have considerable control over how we direct our thinking. Having a realistic understanding of our personal limitations is critical. But *dwelling* on them is always counter-productive. And it's not honoring to God. In general, we should give much more attention to looking for ways to solve problems, than to trying to explain why they can't be remedied. When we're able to make this mental shift, we're often surprised by the difference it makes. We begin to see answers to "impossible" predicaments, and ways to pursue dreams that before had eluded us.

The Benefit of Vision
There's a second characteristic that I believe accounts for Greg Lukens' triumph over his disability, and it's what I would simply call *vision*. Greg is someone with substantial vision. I say this not to be cute; I'd use the same term even if he didn't suffer a visual handicap. By this I mean that Greg has *focus*. He had a clear dream of something he wanted to accomplish with his life, and it was a passionate dream, which fueled his energy and defined how he spent his time. Most important, he focused more upon the results he wanted to achieve than upon the problems that might keep him from getting there.

We shouldn't underestimate the value that a sense of vision can provide for any of us, especially if we feel stuck in a rut and uncertain how to move forward with our life. Having a dream we want to pursue, and establishing goals we want to reach—even if they are very long-term ones—can do wonders to focus our thinking, and to help us find the courage to take otherwise scary steps of faith.

The point is not that God would necessarily expect any of us to build a major business, as Greg has, or to achieve outrageous financial success. Our vision should fit the unique gifts and interests God has given us. Yet having vision can make all the difference in how our potential is realized.

We tend to think that others who've reached certain points in life to which we aspire have done so because they're more talented than we are, or are less cursed with obstacles in their path. Yet when we look closely at these people, we so often find that their potential isn't any greater than our own—perhaps even less. And many of them have had their fair share of setbacks and hurdles to jump along the way. They're where they are not due to unusual talent, but because of focus, persistence, and the simple confidence that they could succeed.

A Simpler Answer Than Anyone Imagined

Consider again David's encounter with Goliath (1 Sam 17). We might assume David succeeded in defeating Goliath because he was more gifted as a warrior than others in Israel then. In fact, quite the opposite was probably true. He was younger than most of the soldiers, and far less experienced in combat. There's no question that many were also experienced with a sling, and some could likely have beaten David in a marksmanship contest.

Yet Goliath had so successfully taunted the Israelite army that every last soldier—from the newest recruit to the king himself—was convinced the giant couldn't be defeated in one-on-one combat. This conclusion had settled in so solidly that a gloomy groupthink prevailed. Most were obviously spending their energy explaining why the problem couldn't be solved, rather than looking for a creative solution.

David undoubtedly benefited from not being a soldier, and

being outside of this defeatist environment. He was by nature an optimist and a problem solver. His attitude wasn't, "here's an impossible predicament," but, "why *can't* this problem be solved?" In that spirit, he reasoned from his past experience to the present: since he had killed bears and lions with a sling as a shepherd, he should be able to defeat even an oversized human opponent this same way. David may well have concluded, too, that by dumbing down his approach—by going into battle without sword or armor, but merely a sling—he could catch Goliath off guard and have an advantage, which is exactly what happened.

What's most encouraging about this episode, is that the solution David came up with to a supposedly impossible problem was *simple*. Amazingly simple. It was so straightforward and obvious, in fact, that it's astonishing no one else had thought of it. But David alone made the connection between his past experience and taking on Goliath. David defeated the giant not because of superior talent but because of superior *attitude*. His faith-inspired thinking allowed him to see connections and a solution that others had missed.

Our View of Christ Makes a Radical Difference

David's example inspires us to realize that problems in our own life that we consider insurmountable may in fact have solutions—even simpler ones than we've imagined. It encourages us also not to be too quick to give up on our personal dreams. It reminds us that attitude more than talent so often makes the difference in what we accomplish, and that our limitations may even work to our benefit when we have a clear goal we want to reach.

As David's life unfolds in Scripture, it becomes clear that one factor more than any other accounted for his exceptional ability to think so constructively. He had a vigorous relationship with God, which affected how he viewed every aspect of life. He sought the Lord constantly, and walked with him continually.

His view of God was also extraordinarily positive. "This I know, that God is for me," David declares in Psalm 56:9. He was certain

God wanted the very best for his life, and was working continually to bring it about. And he focused far more on God's grace and strength, than upon his own limitations and inadequacies. This led him to assume by default that many daunting problems in his life could be solved.

We each will benefit greatly from taking time daily to be alone with Christ, to nurture our relationship with him, and to renew our confidence that he desires the best for us. We should remind ourselves constantly that he is *for* us, and infinitely capable of bringing about his plan for our life. As that conviction sinks in more and more, we'll find it more natural to keep our limitations in proper perspective, and not to let them be the overriding factor as we think toward the future.

Even more important, through walking closely with Christ, we open ourselves to his inspiration, and to what Paul terms "the mind of Christ" about our life (1 Cor 2:16). Nothing helps us more to see beyond our limitations to our true potential, and to find the courage to embrace dreams that are truly right for us.

4

The Triumph of Hope

Deeply-felt hope is the attitude of heart that best opens me to God's provision as I pursue a dream. It is also far more achievable than "mountain-moving faith."

IN THE PREFACE TO HIS LAST BOOK, George Burns wrote that he no longer expected to live an active public life. "I'm still an optimist. But I'm not stupid. That nurse isn't watching me all day to see if my toupee is on straight."[1]

Burns had decided to accept the fact that his life was declining, rather than fight it. A mature step in choosing to live with reality, we might say.

Yet Burns was 100 when he wrote these words. For years he had been an icon of optimism, challenging elderly people not to limit themselves, and speaking often of his burning determination to reach 100. His positive spirit clearly worked for him. He continued to perform stand-up comedy to adoring crowds into his late 90s.

Burns' example brings us to the heart of one of the most challenging questions we face in life. When should we continue to fight—to hold on to the best of life as we know it, and to improve situations in our life—and when is it presumptuous to do so? When is hope our best response to challenges, and when is acceptance the wiser course?

Life often makes this question difficult for us. After my father was hospitalized at 77 with a heart problem so severe it rendered him unable to walk, his cardiologist asked to speak with me. He explained in dismal detail that Dad's condition was dire. When he finally paused, I started to ask him, "Doctor, in the best-case scenario, what are my dad's prospects?" But before I could finish the question, he cut me off, exclaiming, "Mr. Smith, *there is no best-case scenario.* Your father will never walk again nor leave the hospital."

This pronouncement, coming from one of the most respected heart specialists in our region, seemed like a divine oracle. I nearly let go of hope for dad's recovery at that point.

That specialist's opinion, fortunately, wasn't shared by my father, who one month later walked out of the hospital, and went on to live another seven years. He walked and continued to drive his car during most of that time.

My father's experience illustrates a major reason why the hope-vs.-acceptance question is sometimes so difficult. Even when we're justified in continuing to hope and fight, others whom we respect may fail to see the light at the end of our tunnel. They may insist that our situation is beyond hope, and urge us simply to accept reality. Even those who are most qualified to advise us may counsel us in this way.

The challenge can be especially great for an elderly person facing a medical crisis. Dr. Eleanor S. Stewart, a specialist in geriatric medicine, notes that medical professionals often give up too easily when treating older patients.[2] Their health problems are usually more difficult to diagnose than those of younger patients, and many specialists don't invest the time needed to do it precisely. Many are too quick also to assume a patient is too old to respond to treatment effectively.

Stewart cites the case of a 98-year-old man whom she recommended for minor cancer surgery. Following the operation, he was no longer able to walk. His HMO claimed he was too old to benefit from rehabilitation and should move to a nursing home. Stewart insisted, however, that because he had walked into the hospital, he ought to be able to walk out. In the end, Stewart prevailed, and her patient responded well to physical therapy. Her crowning moment of vindication came when she danced with him at his 100th birthday celebration.

The moral of these examples is that we should be extremely slow to give up the fight in matters of life and health. We can be too bullheaded about it, to be sure. The point comes when we do need to accept that a condition is irreversible. Dr. Stewart is just as quick to castigate medical professionals who take heroic measures to preserve the lives of patients who have no reasonable hope of benefiting. Yet we should require abundant evidence before we conclude that a medical problem we or someone else experiences is incurable. Until that point, we should keep the emphasis strongly upon hope.

Hope and Our Personal Dreams

The same point applies with our major life dreams. We shouldn't be quick to let go of dreams that are founded on a good understanding of who we are.

The more I study Scripture, the more I'm impressed with how greatly it encourages us to be optimistic about realizing our personal potential. Scripture pictures God as infinitely compassionate and infinitely powerful—intent on bringing about his best for our life, and fully capable of doing so. It teaches, too, that he has fashioned our personality and influences our desires. We have, in short, a reassuring basis for taking our personal dreams seriously. If we are intent on doing God's will, and are taking care to seek his guidance, we may trust that our dreams are being inspired by him to an important extent. It only makes sense, then, to stay hopeful about achieving them.

This point came home to me forcefully, in a surprising way, when I was searching for a biblical verse to use as a caption for my ministry's web site. I decided to examine those that speak of hope. I typed "hope" into my computer concordance. Stunned by the sheer number of verses that suddenly flashed across my computer screen—about 185 in all—I felt like a divine scroll was unraveling in front of me. Time and again Scripture implores us to "hope in the Lord." It is one of the prominent themes of the Bible.

This biblical emphasis on hoping in God has several thrilling implications for realizing our potential.

• *We not only have permission to dream big about our future, but a mandate.* Hoping in God means, first and foremost, reverencing him intensely and devoting ourselves earnestly to him. Yet it also involves trusting with childlike confidence that he'll take care of all the particulars of our life. We shouldn't minimize what an extraordinary gift it is to us that we're encouraged to exercise this trust. The fact that he has infinite control over all human affairs means that we are, by definition, being urged to think and dream big about our future.

The author of Psalm 146 writes:

Happy is he whose help is the God of Jacob, whose hope is in the LORD his God, who made heaven and earth, the sea, and all that is in them; who keeps faith for ever; who executes justice for the oppressed; who gives food to the hungry. The LORD sets the prisoners free; the LORD opens the eyes of the blind. The LORD lifts up those who are bowed down; the LORD loves the righteous. The LORD watches over the sojourners, he upholds the widow and the fatherless . . . . (Ps 146:5-9 RSV)

The psalmist urges us to hope in the Lord, noting that he is infinitely powerful, having "made heaven and earth, the sea, and all that is in them." He then stresses that God actively works to remedy the most difficult problems a person faces, including political oppression, hunger, imprisonment, blindness, homelessness, and the loss of critical relationships. Hoping in God, then, is not a vague or ethereal exercise. It means nothing less than desiring his help at our greatest points of need.

The fact that it's God's nature to help us with the most difficult challenges we face is an invitation to think big as we plan our life. We *honor* him by coming to understand the gifts and interests he has given us, then establishing significant dreams based upon them. And, apart from compelling evidence that he wants us to abandon any of them, we honor him by continuing to hope eagerly that he'll bring them to pass.

This point is important to stress, for many Christians assume that hoping in God requires us to relinquish all personal ambition and cling to God alone. The biblical concept of hope, however, is almost 180 degrees from this. Hoping in God does mean letting go of aspirations that are contrary to his will. And it means trusting that the greatest blessings in store for us lie not in this life but eternity.

Yet it also involves holding strongly to dreams that relate to realizing our potential in this life. Hoping in this manner is part of exercising good stewardship over the life God has entrusted to us. Far from an option for the Christian, it's a requirement.

• *Hope is achievable.* Another greatly encouraging aspect of hope is that it's an outlook we each have the full potential to experience.

Scripture describes another attitude of confidence in God, which it terms *faith,* and both Jesus and Paul spoke of a quality of faith that can "move mountains" (Mt 17:20, 21:21-22; Mk 11:22-24; I Cor 13:2). Jesus explained that this special level of faith requires us to believe with unbending conviction that he'll carry out what we ask him to do.

Hope, by contrast, doesn't require absolute certainty about an outcome, but merely a strong desire for it, coupled with a conviction that God can and may bring it to pass.

I'm convinced, both from experience and my study of Scripture, that very few Christians ever experience mountain-moving faith. Such unshakable conviction about how God will act is a spiritual gift, which he imparts to only a small number of believers. However, each of us has the capacity not only to hope, but to hope *substantially.* And the quality of our hope can actually grow, and its intensity increase, over time.

• *Hope works.* The fact that we have such great potential for experiencing hope is especially thrilling because it benefits us in such remarkable ways. Its effect on our well-being is considerable. As our hope increases, we're more consistently happy, and our health is likely to improve. We think more clearly, plan and work more effectively toward our future. Others are more naturally drawn to us as well, and more inclined to help us reach our goals.

Even more important are hope's spiritual benefits. By hoping in God, we relate to him in a way that Scripture extols. We're better able to understand his guidance in this state of mind. And we allow him greater freedom to influence both our thinking and our circumstances in ways that move us toward his best.

There is, in short, efficacy in hope. This is why the psalmist counsels, "Be strong and take heart, all you who hope in the LORD" (Ps. 31:24).

The Dynamics of Hope

As Christians, then, we have a sound basis for thinking big as we plan our life, and for staying determined to reach goals that are based on a good understanding of how God has gifted and motivated us. We should keep the accent strongly upon hope, even when our journey toward a dream takes considerably longer than we've anticipated.

Several further dynamics of the biblical attitude of hope are helpful to keep in mind as we strive to constructively anticipate our future. These also help to explain how we can keep hope and acceptance in healthy balance.

• *Cherishing strong hope for the future is not incompatible with staying highly content in the present.* One of the most refreshing aspects of the outlook we're talking about is that it blends hope and acceptance remarkably. We're encouraged to dream heartily about our future and to stay intent on reaching our goals. Yet never does Scripture suggest that our worth as a person depends upon achieving them. Our well-being doesn't have to hinge on our success; what we accomplish doesn't justify our existence.

And because of the supreme trust we're urged to place in God's uncanny timing, we have permission to enjoy the present fully, and never to feel we're acquiescing or "settling" by doing so. The sheer joy that comes from relating to God personally brings immense pleasure into our present as well, even as we live with unfulfilled dreams.

We're able, in short, to have the best of both worlds: high hope for the future, and joyful acceptance of things as they are now.

• *Our hope for the future should be broad-based, not narrowly-focused.* One of the secrets of nurturing hope that honors God and respects the potential he has given us, is learning to hold strongly to important dreams without fixating on specific ways they must be accomplished.

If we have a strong desire to be married, for instance, we're justified in holding firm to this dream for as long as it takes to find a good opportunity. Nothing in Scripture requires us to let go of this hope simply because we have reached a certain age, or suffered a certain number of disappointments. A friend of mine enjoyed her first courtship in her late sixties; it was also her first dating relationship ever.

But where many of us push the envelope too greatly is in clinging to the hope of marrying *a specific person* beyond a realistic point. If a relationship opens with someone we would like to marry, we should stay optimistic about marrying this person for as long as our hope is reasonable. But if we find that he or she isn't willing to marry us, or isn't suitable for us, we should determine to let this particular dream go. Yet this doesn't mean we should abandon our hope for marriage itself.

It's here that we have an exceptional opportunity for growing in faith. We may trust that God, who has made us each exceedingly resilient, is fully capable of redirecting our affection to someone else, who will likely prove to be an even better match for us.

We should follow this same pattern when choosing to hope or accept in other areas. If there's a career we want to pursue that fits our potential well, we should hold fast to the dream of succeeding in it, for as long as it takes. But we need to be flexible about *where* we work. If a specific job opportunity doesn't open to us, or a certain geographical region is closed, we should accept that these doors are shut and move on.

But we shouldn't let such limited setbacks take on more importance than they deserve. They shouldn't deter us from our long-term goal of succeeding in this profession. The key is to keep our career dream as broad-based as possible.

• *Hope inspires prayer.* While it's vital that we dream big about our future, it's just as important that we not simply be "dreamers." Hope, even for accomplishing legitimate goals, can take on an unhealthy dimension. Some people take too much refuge in a fantasy world built around hope, which deters them from being responsible. The hope that Christ inspires moves us to take significant responsibility, and in two important ways.

One is through prayer. Scripture encourages us constantly to express our needs to God in prayer, and to continue praying until he answers. While plenty of mystery surrounds prayer, Scripture couldn't be clearer that prayer does influence God. He limits much of what he does to what we choose to ask him to accomplish. He focuses his work in this manner both to give us a sense of partnership with him in his mission on earth, and to deepen our dependence upon him.

Hope is what inspires in us the ability to pray effectively. Whenever we find the courage to pray boldly, or the tenacity to persist in prayer, it's only because we have strong hope that God will grant our request. Without hope, meaningful prayer is impossible. But when we deeply desire to achieve a goal, and believe it's within the realm of God's possibilities for us, then we're in a state of mind to pray in a way that makes a difference.

Having hope doesn't *guarantee* we'll give the attention to prayer that we should. This will only happen if we're convinced prayer is necessary. The important thing for each of us is to remind ourselves often that prayer isn't just a cathartic exercise, but an essential step toward realizing our potential. We should then dwell on what we desire God to do, and let our hope for that inspire us to pray earnestly.

• *Hope inspires action.* When God's Spirit inspires hope within us, it also stimulates us to take important steps toward realizing our dreams. It's here that the hope Scripture encourages differs most clearly from mere wishful thinking. Of course, trusting in Christ sometimes requires we do nothing *but* hope. Our responsibility is to wait patiently in faith for him to act.

Yet when there's a clear course of action we can take toward reaching a goal, it's usually best to assume God wants us to take a step of faith. It's time for us to take initiative.

In Jeremiah 29:11, God declares, "For I know the plans I have for you . . . plans to prosper you and not to harm you, plans to give you a hope and a future." Here God assures the Israelites that he will provide plentifully for them, and urges them to stay hopeful about their future. Yet he precedes this cherished promise with an exhortation to take responsibility:

> "Build houses and settle down; plant gardens and eat what they produce. Marry and have sons and daughters; find wives for your sons and give your daughters in marriage . . . . Also, seek the peace and prosperity of the city to which I have carried you in exile. Pray to the LORD for it, because if it prospers, you too will prosper." (Jer 29:5-7)

Because of the hope they have in him, God tells the Israelites, they should take initiative to improve their lives and to remedy their most pressing needs.

Most interesting is that the Jews were in *Babylon* at this time. They were highly depressed over being deported there, and saw no good in their present situation whatever. They had every reason to believe they couldn't be successful pursuing their personal dreams there—that the doors were bolted shut against them. Yet God tells them to throw caution to the winds, and to take courageous steps to rebuild their lives. By prompting them to take this initiative, he implies he'll give them many successes as they move forward.

Which brings us back to our question of hope vs. acceptance. While there are times when it's essential we accept that a door is closed, we can give up too easily. Like the Israelites, we look at our circumstances and conclude that they rule out our possibly achieving our dreams—so why bother even to try?

Yet we don't know the mind of God, nor how he might provide for us if we venture forward. If there is at least a small step we can take to begin moving toward a goal, we usually do best to err on the side of hope, and to put our life in motion. We exercise greater faith by taking initiative, than by merely "accepting reality" and sitting still.

Beyond the What Ifs

One Friday evening when our son Nate was a young college student, he had an unforgettable experience. He and his girlfriend set out to drive to her high school prom, at a Bethesda hotel about forty-five minutes from our home. About halfway there, the alternator in Nate's car gave out, and his engine died. He remembered that an old family friend lived in the neighborhood next to the highway where they were stranded. They began walking around that community looking for the familiar house, Nate in a black tux and his friend in a stunning evening dress.

A woman driving home from work stopped and offered to help. She drove them down street after street, but they were unable to locate our friend's home. Finally, she offered to let them take *her* car to the prom. Never mind that she had never met either of them

before. These two young people were in a bind, and she was determined to help.

Nate and his girlfriend arrived at the prom—a bit late, but with
a story to tell that became the talk of the evening. Their experience
of such unspeakable human kindness and, I believe, divine inter-
vention, made it an evening to forever remember for them.

Their odyssey that night is similar to what our experience so
often is as we begin moving toward a personal dream. Problems we
fear sometimes do occur. Even worst-case scenarios. What we can't
predict is how God will protect us and provide for us at such times.
And the uncanny ways that he bails us out of the worst predicaments only add to the richness of our journey toward a cherished
goal.

Which is to say that we shouldn't be deterred from pursuing a
dream by the "what ifs." If a goal fits our potential well, we should
go for it, trusting that God will help us with the most difficult challenges that arise. Finding God's best for our life almost always requires that we take some steps where it does feel for all the world
like we're throwing caution to the winds. It's only in this adven-
turesome spirit that we're able to make good judgments about doors
being open or closed.

Or in the words of Reinhold Neibuhr's immortal prayer (and
slightly paraphrased): to have the wisdom to know what we can
change and what we can't, the courage to pursue the one, and the
serenity to accept the other.

* * * * * * * *

In chapter two I stressed that desiring a dream strongly and being
available to pursue it put you in a position of strength from the
moment you take that dream on. In a similar way, hope strengthens
your position, by encouraging you to act and pray, by inspiring others to help you, and by making you more alert to God's guidance. I
hope that by this point in our study you're realizing what an unspeakable gift it is simply to have a dream that's propelling your
life, and are feeling greater courage to think big about your future.

Still, there's a nagging question that needs to be more carefully addressed. How, after all, can I embrace a dream passionately, yet still be properly thankful to Christ for my life as it is now? Doesn't contentment in Christ rule out striving to improve my circumstances? In the next chapter we'll look at how we can be continually grateful to God in our current state, yet still be motivated for positive change.

5

Contentment and Motivation

I can be happy in the Lord and grateful for my life as it is now, yet still motivated to improve it in different ways. Dreaming big isn't incompatible with being content in Christ.

A YOUNG MAN ONCE PHONED ME to share an idea he had for a book. He had come to the point in his marriage where he was happy, Gerald explained—content with a situation that used to annoy him. This new horizon was such a breakthrough that he wanted to write about it. He felt he had a liberating message for others— that by accepting unwelcome circumstances, in marriage and in life, they too can learn to be content and happy.

I commended Gerald for his experience of growth. From the little I knew about him, his attitude change seemed healthy, and evidence of God's healing. Normally, I would have left it at that.

But Gerald wanted to write about his milestone—to explore all the nuances. And so I asked him to consider a question: Is contentment always *good* for us? Does God always want us to accept unpleasant situations in our life unreflectively, or does he want us to work at changing some of them?

And are we ever likely to take steps to grow or to improve our life, unless we're dissatisfied with some aspect of it? Doesn't God use discontent in positive ways to motivate us? Is it ever possible for us to a have a dream igniting our life—and enough passion to reach it—unless we're unhappy with our current circumstances in certain ways?

It seemed to me, in short, that contentment and discontent both play vital roles in our lives. Whether my observations challenged Gerald or irritated him, I don't know, for I never heard from him again. Our discussion did challenge *me*, however, to give more serious thought to this matter.

Can We Be Too Content?

If you've been a Christian for any length of time, you've heard plenty of talk about the importance of contentment and thankfulness. Sermons, Sunday School lessons, books and articles stress the message: be thankful for all your difficulties, rejoice in every circumstance. We should learn to be content with what we have, and happy with our lot in life. If we're suffering an unpleasant situation, we're more typically admonished to "accept God's will" than encouraged to change our circumstances.

Scripture indeed has much to say about the value of contentment. Paul lauds it as a virtue in his own life, declaring, "for I have learned to be content whatever the circumstances. I know what it is to be in need, and I know what it is to have plenty. I have learned the secret of being content in any and every situation, whether well fed or hungry, whether living in plenty or in want" (Phil 4:11-12). Elsewhere he notes that he was content with his possessions, as long as he had food and clothing (1 Tim 6:6-8).

In a similar vein, the writer of Hebrews counsels, "Keep your lives free from the love of money and be content with what you have, because God has said, 'Never will I leave you; never will I forsake you'" (Heb 13:5).

Scripture likewise stresses our need for thankfulness. Paul urges the Thessalonians, "give thanks in all circumstances, for this is God's will for you in Christ Jesus" (1 Thes 5:18). And he instructs the Colossians, "be thankful . . . with gratitude in your hearts to God. And whatever you do, whether in word or deed, do it all in the name of the Lord Jesus, giving thanks to God the Father through him" (Col 3:15-17). And he tells the Philippians, "Rejoice in the Lord always. I will say it again: Rejoice!" (Phil 4:4).

In many other ways, Scripture encourages us to appreciate the benefits of our difficult circumstances, and to make our most earnest effort to be happy in the Lord as we endure them. "We rejoice in our sufferings, knowing that suffering produces endurance, and endurance produces character, and character produces hope" (Rom 5:3 RSV). "Rejoice that you participate in the sufferings of Christ, so that you may be overjoyed when his glory is revealed" (1 Pet 4:13). And Paul notes graphically how hardships he suffered helped him better empathize with the misfortunes of others (2 Cor 1:3-7).

Taken by themselves, these passages might seem to be saying that contentment and thankfulness are the end of the story for the Christian. We should strive to be happy with our life as it is, and to regard both welcome and unwelcome situations as God's will. And we should assume that any frustration we feel is Satan's attempt to destroy our joy and to tempt us to act selfishly.

However . . .

Scripture also shows that *discontent* sometimes plays a redemptive role in the Christian's life. To note a few examples:

• In 1 Corinthians 7, Paul teaches that dissatisfaction with being unmarried is an important reason to consider marrying. If I'm truly content being single, I should stay unattached, Paul advises. But if I long for the benefits of marriage, and my sexual need is strong, then I should marry—if a suitable opportunity presents itself. "It is better to marry than to burn with passion" (v. 9).

Discontentment with singleness, then, is part of the guidance God gives us to marry.

• The Israelites became open to leaving Egypt, and were able to embrace the vision of relocating, because they so greatly disdained their life in Egypt. At times, though, when they encountered hardships while marching toward Canaan, they longed to return to Egypt. They complained bitterly to Moses, adding substantial burden to his leadership. On these occasions, disenchantment with their former life of slavery wasn't strong enough! Abhorrence of that state was *healthy* for them, and a necessary part of the emotional drive God used to propel them toward Canaan.

• Paul spoke of being content with his possessions. But when he spoke of his accomplishments, he expressed strong discontent. At one point he deemed them "rubbish," declaring that he must "press on" (Phil 3:4-14).

• At one point during Elijah's tenure as Israel's chief prophet, his disciples grew frustrated with the limitations of their living and working quarters. "See, the place where we dwell under your charge is too small for us," they explain to Elijah (2 Ki 6:1 RSV). Far from rebuking them for being ungrateful, Elijah encourages them to take steps to expand their personal space, and then helps them do it. The passage implies that the disciples' concern was appropriate, and that their discontentment led to an improved environment for their work and study.

• Then there is James' enlightening instruction on prayer: "Is any one among you suffering? Let him pray. Is anyone cheerful? Let him sing praise" (Jas 5:13 RSV). When we're happy with our life, James says, we should sing praise to God—exactly the sort of advice we'd expect from a Christian teacher. But, perhaps surprisingly, he says nothing here about praising God when times are hard. Not that James would have thought it inappropriate to do so; in the beginning of his epistle he exhorts us to rejoice in our trials and to appreciate how they enhance our growth. But here his concern is to urge us to plead for God's assistance when we're suffering.

The benefits that come to us from thanking and praising God are inexpressible. Yet we also benefit remarkably from praying for his help. It increases our dependence on him, and our humble awareness that certain welcome outcomes result from his action and not our own. We also experience a treasured sense of partnership with Christ through petitioning him—a camaraderie that Scripture understands as part of the abundant life he gives us. And prayers of petition are *necessary* for us to enjoy some of God's most welcome blessings.

James' counsel, indeed, mandates us to pray for God's help when we need it. By urging us to pray when we're "suffering," James certainly has in mind any situation where we're frustrated or unhappy. The corollary is most interesting: without some discontentment, we're not likely to pray as fully or effectively as we should.

Common Sense

Common sense also tells us that discontent is part of what drives us anytime we take a major step with our life. Positive motivation inspires us then as well. If I seek a new job, for instance, it's likely because I'm (a) attracted to a new opportunity, and (b) wanting to escape certain factors in my current job. Without this negative drive, I'm unlikely to find enough steam to embrace the positive goal of finding new employment.

W. Clement Stone had a name for this negative motivation: "inspirational dissatisfaction." In his classic self-help manual, *The Success System That Never Fails*, Stone argues that discontent is a vital life-force, giving us both the insight and the impetus for needed change. Inspirational dissatisfaction well describes this essential role frustration plays in our experience, Clement explains. And if we can learn to expect life to be offering us inspirational dissatisfaction, we'll be more alert to the indispensable guidance our negative feelings may be providing us. They may be a window into how God has created us and into new directions he wants us to take.[1]

Having such a term for discontentment's beneficial side is indeed tremendously helpful. Making it part of our vocabulary helps us think in terms of life's giving us vital guidance through unwelcome circumstances. We become more alert to the possible insight

God may be providing us through them.

Being Content *and* Motivated

It was obvious enough to me when I spoke with Gerald that contentment and discontent both play an essential role in our Christian
walk; and Stone's book, which I read later, helped to confirm this
conviction. What was less clear to me, as I mulled this issue, is how
we can be discontented with a situation yet still thankful. Are we
simply dealing with a paradox here? Or can we say in a clear and
helpful way how these two attitudes ought to relate? One day the
answer dawned on me—not as a thunderous epiphany, but more
like the two-by-four to the side of the head!

To say it simply: Scripture never calls us to be content *with*
every circumstance in our life but *in* every circumstance. Thus Paul's
clear language: "I have learned in whatever situation I am to be
content" (Phil 4:11 ESV). Had he said he was content *with* every
situation, his meaning would be radically different—and this *is* how
many Christians understand his statement. Yet Paul clearly was not
content with every situation in his life, and he strove to change
many of them. But he had learned how to be content *in* every one of
them, and in spite of many circumstances that were hard for him.

Fueling this "in spite of" contentment for Paul was a deep sense
of Christ's peace and presence, constantly comforting him in his
challenges. Paul was also keenly aware of certain benefits his difficult experiences provided him—including:

- the stimulus to grow, and lean more fully on Christ (2 Cor
12:7-10)
- the opportunity to develop greater empathy for others going through similar challenges (2 Cor 1:3-7)
- other serendipities and silver linings, such as open doors
for ministry (Phil 1:12-14).

Thus, Paul on the one hand could be profoundly thankful for how
God would bless him through his difficult circumstances, yet still
feel free to strive to change and improve them. If the setting wasn't

good for ministry in one town, for instance, he would simply move on to another. And during his lengthy imprisonment, detailed in the latter chapters of Acts, Paul exhausted every appeal in his effort to be released.

What we learn from Paul, and from the entire teaching of Scripture, is that we're not expected to be giddily happy about every circumstance in our life, nor are we expected to passively accept every unwelcome situation. There is a contentment—in fact, a joy nothing short of elation—that's possible for us in our most trying predicaments, and in spite of them. It springs from Christ's presence and peace, and from recognizing the potential benefits our unwanted circumstances can bring us. At the same time, though, God expects us to give attention to our negative feelings, to consider them carefully, and to recognize that through them he may be providing us important inspiration for change.

And that is enormously good news. We can know there is purpose to our unpleasant circumstances beyond what we've probably imagined. How, then, can we know for certain how God wants us to respond to a particular unwelcome situation? Does he want us to work at accepting it, and does he wish to change us so that we learn to live with it peacefully? Or is he using it to stimulate us to look at what we can do to improve our life—and if so, what action does he want us to take?

The answer to this question boils down to a simple practical principal: If there is something I can clearly do to remedy an unpleasant situation, or to improve it—and without jeopardizing my commitments to others or my obligations to them—then I should do it. I should see it as a matter of stewardship to do what I obviously can to improve my life. But if I'm locked in to the unwelcome situation—through a commitment I've made, or through my obligations to others, or through the force of circumstances—then I should strive to accept it, and to recognize as many benefits in it as possible.

Of course, in many cases we're between these extremes. We

have to continue to live with a frustrating situation for some time, as we take steps to change it. So it's a matter of living in both of these worlds at once.

But we always find Scripture putting the emphasis on being proactive, and on being good stewards of our lives. We're never expected to accept an unhappy situation passively if we have the chance to alter it.

We're expected also to take those major steps that help us better realize our personal potential. Which brings us back to the critical need for our personal dreams. Inspirational dissatisfaction is part of the process that will help us establish a dream and find the motivation to pursue it. We will, in short, usually have a mix of positive and negative drives moving us to follow a dream. In the next section, we'll refine this concept more carefully, and look at how to determine which of the different dreams we may entertain best fit us, and are most worthy of embracing wholeheartedly. With that understanding, we can then move to look at setting goals and getting a dream in motion.

II

Embracing the
Right Dreams

6

Looking Inward and Looking Outward

*I establish those dreams that are most appropriate for me
by matching my gifts and aspirations with needs and
opportunities in the world. While looking in both these
directions is critical, the insight that comes from knowing
myself is, over time, most important.*

IN SEEKING GOD'S WILL, is my primary responsibility to consider how Christ has made me, and then look for situations that best fit my gifts and interests? Or is it to try to understand where the greatest areas of human need lie and do my best to relate to them? Do I find the will of God more reliably by looking inward or by looking outward?

This issue is much more than an academic one for many of us. Consider the case of Chris, a third-year college student in pre-med studies. He has a heart for people, and earnestly wants his life to accomplish something of value for Christ. Since elementary school Chris has dreamed of becoming a medical missionary. This vocation would allow him to meet critical needs of people, and to share the Gospel openly as well. He has locked in to this dream for so long that it seems like a calling and mandate upon his life.

College has been a harsh reality check for Chris. Even though he has worked hard, he hasn't done well in the science courses essential for med school. He has done well in humanities courses, however, and superbly in art and drama. Most significant, Chris has discovered a strong talent for acting, and has played the lead role in several school plays.

Now, well into his third college year, Chris is concluding he'd most like to pursue an acting career, and he has the skill and drive to do so. Yet he fears he wouldn't contribute nearly as greatly to people's needs or the work of Christ in this career as in medical missions. He wonders if he's giving up on his long-time goal too easily. Should he simply work harder in science, and redouble his efforts to get into med school?

For Chris, the central issue is whether to base his understanding of God's will on looking outward or looking inward. Looking outward tells him he should follow a career in medical missions at all costs, for it seems to be where he can make the most obvious impact for Christ. Looking inward tells him he's really more cut out for acting. Is it possible God is giving him guidance through this discovery about himself? Or is it Satan's way of tempting him to turn away from God's best?

Not a few of us experience this same conflict at various times in our own decisions. The choices before us may not contrast as strongly as in Chris's case. Yet they may leave us similarly confused about God's will.

How often it seems we face this dilemma in our major life choices: At one extreme is an option we see as a golden opportunity to help people and have a ministry. At the other extreme is an opportunity more in line with our natural gifts and interests. And so often there seems to be a frustrating distance between these two extremes.

We confront the inward-outward issue not only in vocational choices, but in many other areas. Opportunities to serve in our churches so often seem to pit one option, where the needs are gaping, against another that better fits our talents and temperament, but where the needs are less pressing. We typically face this issue in some of our avocational choices as well.

Advice That Confuses

More often than not, the advice we hear in Christian circles is that looking outward is more important in finding God's will than looking inward. Consider the popular adage we hear so often: "God wants your availability, not your ability." While this may be reverent advice on one level, it's too often taken to mean that our abilities are *unimportant* to God. Our responsibility before him is simply to look for needs and fill them, trusting that he will give us the ability necessary to meet them.

Some Christians even assume we best fulfill God's will by taking on responsibility we're *clearly* not gifted to handle. By doing so, they argue, we compel ourselves to trust Christ to make us effective, and we best position ourselves to function by faith.

This outlook is obviously reverent and well-intentioned. Yet does it accord with biblical teaching on guidance? Where does Scripture put the emphasis in seeking God's will—upon looking outward or looking inward?

Balancing Gifts and Needs

Clearly these two concerns are never mutually exclusive. We are always responsible to look outward and inward at the same time. Scripture prods us constantly to the most thoroughgoing concern for the burdens of other people. We're called to do nothing less than sacrifice our life for the needs of others. Paul tells us in graphic language to consider our life a "living sacrifice," in Romans 12:1.

Yet in the same breath he says emphatically that we must have a good understanding of the life we're sacrificing, and give ourselves accordingly. "Have a sane estimate of your capabilities," Paul declares in Romans 12:3 (Phillips). We're to develop as realistic a self-understanding as possible. We're called to appreciate the distinctive gifts and characteristics God has given us, and to be good stewards of them.

Sensible decisions to invest ourselves, then, can only be made as we match everything we know about ourselves with everything we're able to learn about the needs of others and opportunities to serve.

Further, our self-understanding is never achieved merely by looking inward. It only emerges through our involvement with others. If I decide that I'll never do anything for Christ until I'm certain what my gifts are, I'll wait forever! I discover my gifts, and my whole range of strengths and limitations, only over time, as I do my best to understand the needs of people around me and respond to them, then do my best to gauge where I'm being most effective. This will clearly mean some bold experimenting.

As a new Christian, I had no perception I could teach. Late one Saturday evening, a pastor from my church phoned and asked if I would spell him in the college Sunday school class the next morning. Though very reluctant, I agreed to give it a try, nearly certain my performance would be miserable. By the end of the class, though, I sensed that, in spite of many deficiencies, the Lord had used me. Communication had occurred. And to my surprise, I had greatly enjoyed the experience.

The need for experimenting never ceases in our lives. We never reach the point where we have the right to think we've fully understood our gifts or reached all our creative horizons. God is full of surprises and, at any point in life—even older age, may show us we have the capacity to do something we'd always thought was out of our range of potential (Ps 92:12-14).

I knew a woman who, as a middle-aged homemaker, suffered terribly from migraine headaches. She was asked to help with a ministry to disadvantaged children living in one of Washington, D.C.'s most dangerous neighborhoods—a task you'd imagine would give a middle-class, suburban woman a migraine. Through she had no previous experience in social work or cross-cultural ministry, she agreed to try. To her amazement, she not only was highly effective, but her headaches disappeared. Her experience demonstrates dramatically how courageous experimenting can sometimes shed surprising light on our potential.

Following Our Gifts

God, then, takes us through a number of pilgrimages in the Christian life through which we discover our potential more fully. Yet he also brings us to plateaus in our self-understanding, where we recognize that we clearly have certain talent and are motivated to use it. These are the points where we're most likely to conclude that our life isn't reflecting our gifts and motivational pattern as fully as it could. We may envision certain changes that would bring our life more into line with our God-given potential.

It's here that the conflict between looking inward and looking outward can become most severe. It may seem that doing what we're most gifted and motivated to do won't meet the needs of others as well as some other alternative that barely taps our potential.

And it's here that I'm comfortable saying the emphasis should be given to our gifts. We should feel not just a freedom but a mandate to follow their direction. Again, I take my cue from Romans 12. Amplifying further what it means to live our lives sacrificially, Paul exhorts us to be about the business of using gifts that we're confident we possess:

> Through the grace of God we have different gifts. If our gift is preaching, let us preach to the limit of our vision. If it is serving others let us concentrate on our service; if it is teaching let us give all we have to our teaching; and if our gift be the stimulating of the faith of others let us set ourselves to it. (Rom 12:6-7 Phillips)

As we come to understand that God has gifted us in a certain way, Paul is saying, we have a responsibility to invest our life at that point. Concentrating on our gifts will mean that we have to take our hands off of other worthwhile things we could be doing. This freedom to focus our time and talent is one of the wonderful benefits of being part of the body of Christ, where God calls others to carry out the work we are unable to do.

The Light That We Have

I'm also comfortable saying that as a general principle over our lifetime, we should give more weight in our big decisions to our self-understanding than to the more abstract question of the needs of other people. I say this with caution, frankly groping for the best words to express the thought, for the danger of hardening our hearts to the needs of others in the interest of doing our own thing is always there. God expects us to be continually pliable and willing to go beyond our boundaries for the sake of helping others.

But I say what I say for the sake of *stewardship*. For what we can know of ourselves—our gifts and abilities, personality traits, energy level, etc.—though always a provisional understanding, is still the most clear and certain knowledge we have this side of eternity on which to base our important choices. And there's an abundance of Scriptural teaching telling us to take this information seriously as a vital indication of how God wants us to spend our lives.

We must also recognize in all humility that all we can understand by looking outward is extremely limited. Our minds are simply too small to comprehend more than a minute portion of all that God is doing in the world. Even when it comes to judging the results of our own work, we see only the faintest tip of the iceberg. We simply can't see enough of the total picture merely by looking outward to judge objectively how and where we'll be most effective for Christ. Understanding our own gifts and creative interests will give us the most important clue.

How It Applies

I don't pretend to know God's will for Chris. He may gain many new insights into his potential in the months and years ahead that throw new light on his career direction. Yet if he continues to perceive that acting is the vocation he's most gifted and motivated to be in, he should feel great freedom to follow that career, trusting that God will give him a significant ministry within it. And he shouldn't assume he's sacrificing a higher calling for a lower one by this choice. Chris may be confident he's fulfilling the Lord's highest calling for him if he's living his life in light of how God has designed it.

For each of us, the critical question is how God has gifted and energized us personally. With a good understanding there, we'll be in the best position to consider how to invest ourselves for the needs of a hurting world. Ultimately, our life will be of greatest benefit to others when we're being the individual God has created us to be.

Keeping this principle strongly in mind will help us take hold of dreams that reflect God's best intentions for our life. And it will help us let go of any that may be based too greatly on a sense of duty, or a need to rescue others, rather than a good understanding of our true potential.

There's another factor that can lead us to embrace the wrong dreams, and it's an unhealthy urge to emulate the gifts and accomplishments of others we admire. We'll look at this problem, and at how to avoid it, in the next chapter.

7

Beating the Comparison Trap

Dreams I embrace will most likely succeed if I base them upon God's unique design of my own life; they will most likely fail if I base them upon the gifts or accomplishments of others.

IT WAS THE FIRST TIME EVER that I'd heard a Charlie Hunter song. The jazz instrumental, *Someday We'll All Be Free*, which Hunter plays with only bass accompaniment, melted me, and I phoned the radio station at once to find out who the guitarist on this recording was.[1] I felt immediately that this was a song I wanted to perform on guitar myself. While I knew it would stretch me, I was sure I could learn it with some effort, and that the challenge would be good for me. Although I'd never heard of Hunter, I was pleased to find the CD in a store the next day, and purchased it.

If you happen to be a Charlie Hunter fan, you're already chuckling, for you know where this story is heading.

I was surprised enough to find that Hunter plays an eight-string guitar, unlike the six-string model picked by most ordinary mortals. I was astounded to find that no bass player is listed in the album credits, even though I was certain I'd heard one on the radio.

Of course, Hunter could have dubbed in the bass part himself. But the album is produced by Blue Note, a purist jazz label that would never stoop to such studio trickery.

It couldn't be, I thought.

It was.

Hunter plays both the lead guitar part and the bass part on this song—as he does on every selection on the album—*at the same time*. He picks the guitar portion on the high strings, the bass portion on the low strings. And he plays complex, nuanced lines, that any guitarist or bassist would be proud to play as individual parts by themselves.

Hunter covers them both at once.

While I've witnessed many guitarists, like Chet Atkins, who can play multiple guitar lines at the same time, I've never encountered one who can play bass and guitar parts simultaneously—a skill I hadn't previously thought possible. I was delighted to discover Hunter's unusual talent, and his music is truly inspiring.

Yet this discovery had a demoralizing effect on me, for I knew if I practiced a lifetime, I couldn't come close to matching his remarkable skill. That realization dampened my enthusiasm for doing what I can do—which is to learn the guitar portion of the song I'd so enjoyed.

Finally it dawned on me that I was falling in to the same rut I warn others to avoid. I was letting Hunter's talent be a benchmark for judging my own. This envious comparing led me to devalue my own talent, and went well beyond healthy humility, for it sapped my motivation to take a step of growth that was within my reach.

Embracing the Right Dreams

Each of us is far more capable of setting significant goals and achieving them than we normally realize. Dreams that seem impossible may even be much more within our reach than we imagine. The secret lies in how we focus our thinking. Beginning with the premise that the problems we encounter can be solved, then dwelling on finding solutions, can make a radical difference. This approach to life is at the heart of what one writer has termed "the magic of thinking big."[2]

This isn't to imply that *any* dream we wish to achieve can be accomplished through such positive thinking. Thinking big has it limits, which are vital to respect. The dreams we establish and the goals we set need to reflect the potential God has given us, and his unique design of our life. If we tread too far outside this arena, we can end up thinking big in a manner that works against us. We can lock in to goals that don't fit us well, and even devote considerable energy to attempting to reach them.

It's easy to fall into what psychologists term an "idealized self-image." Rather than base our dreams upon an honest understanding of how God has fashioned us, we base them upon some glorified idea of what we ought to do.

We noted in the last chapter a common way this happens: we base a dream too greatly on the needs of others, without weighing our own potential carefully enough. Yet such idealized dreaming often springs, too, from unfair comparisons we make of ourselves with others. We esteem someone else's talent, or success, or possessions or benefits they enjoy, and decide we would be better off in their position. We may even establish a major dream, and stake our self-worth, on our ability to match their success. Yet this grass-is-greener mentality is bound to frustrate us, especially if our gifts and potential differ significantly from theirs.

As an avid guitarist, I've often fallen into this comparison trap when listening to other players. It was, of course, outlandish that I gave even a passing thought to how my musical ability stacks up against Charlie Hunter's. There are probably not a half-dozen people on our planet who can perform his musical feat. Yet this is how our psyche works. We instinctively compare ourselves with others in countless ways we have no business doing.

The process is most insidious when we establish major dreams based on others' potential rather than our own. While it's commendable that we have vision, we're basing it on God's design of others' lives, not ours. This idealizing can leave us greatly dispirited if we're unable to live up to the accomplishments of others we esteem. It can rob us of the motivation to take our own potential seriously, and to work toward goals we actually can reach. It can also incite us to strive unreasonably hard to accomplish goals that aren't appropriate for us.

We each face a formidable challenge in reaping the potential we genuinely do have. Each of us needs to strive to understand as clearly as we can how God has fashioned us. We need a good grasp of our talents, capabilities, interests and energy level. In light of this understanding, we need to forge dreams and goals that fit us, and pursue them earnestly. Momentum is critical to succeeding at them.

Yet we can try too hard at any point. Establishing a pace that's right for us makes all the difference.

It can help to remember the dynamics of flight. An airplane needs to be moving at a reasonable speed to gain lift and become airborne. But if, once in flight, the pilot raises the trajectory too high, the plane will lose its thrust and descend.

This is a good parallel to realizing our potential. We need goals, and we need to be moving toward them at a reasonable pace to achieve them. Yet if we raise the trajectory too high—by setting unrealistic goals, or by pushing ourselves too hard to reach them—we will "crash and burn." Keeping balance in the process is essential.

The secret to this balanced visionary thinking is to base our goals, and our pace toward them, upon our own potential, not others'. As simple a principle as this is, it's challenging to follow.

And it's challenging not only in career and lifestyle choices, but with relationships. Having ideals for our friendships, dating relationships and whom we would marry, is essential. Yet these need to be based upon our genuine relationships needs. They should take into account not only our need for companionship, but for growth—

remembering that God uses the rough edges of relationships to teach us how to better love and care for others.

We too often base our relationship ideals on others' experiences. We esteem certain relationships others enjoy, and these become the standard for us. We should strive to understand where our own relationship needs are different, and base our choices on what is uniquely right for us.

Help from David's Example

Scripture offers us a wealth of insight and inspiration for this process of establishing our ideals and dreams. Some of the most helpful enlightenment comes from examples of those who either succeeded or failed at the task. Once again, the life of David, the Old Testament king, is especially helpful to consider, for he set many stunning goals and succeeded in reaching them. Yet he also overdid it at times and fell flat on his face. His life is an intriguing mix of both dimensions of thinking big.

David was, overall, an exceptionally gifted visionary thinker. His decision as a very young man to fight Goliath is one of the most impressive examples in Scripture of someone thinking big in a constructive way (1 Sam 17). Although an extremely high-stakes venture for David, it was suitable given his gifts and experience, as we've noted. As a shepherd he had, with a sling, killed wild animals that had threatened his flock. He had developed a simple strategy for defeating a fierce opponent, and from experience learned that it worked. He had also discovered he had the presence of mind to carry it out at those moments he was under attack and his life hung in the balance.

While fighting Goliath meant taking on a new and greater challenge, David had good reason to believe he possessed both the skill and temperament for it (1 Sam 17:34-37). The rewards for succeeding were also immense: the glory of God was at stake, and a nation of people stood to benefit from his action. He and his family would benefit in major ways as well. Some risk, then, was more than justified.

As grandiose as David's brothers thought his dream of fighting Goliath was, it was in fact appropriate for him, and he proved it with the first shot of his sling. David's encounter with Goliath symbolizes his approach to life during his years as a warrior and his decades as king. He was an uncanny optimist and a master at thinking big. He had instinctively good judgment for recognizing good options for himself and his people, and he took many ingenious steps that successfully brought them about. His example inspires us to see the bigger possibilities for our own life and to go for them.

Yet David didn't always get it right. He made some major blunders at times, which sprang from thinking too grandiosely. In each case, David probably became too obsessed with trying to match the accomplishments of others.

On one notorious occasion, he decided to take a census of Israel, a step that brought God's wrath upon the nation (2 Sam 24, 1 Chron 21). Although Scripture doesn't reveal precisely why taking the census angered God, it must have been that David was seeking more information than he needed to govern by faith. He undoubtedly wanted to know how Israel compared population-wise with other nations, and especially how Israel's military strength stacked up against other countries'. Instead, he should have simply trusted in faith that God had given Israel exactly the people and resources needed to carry out his purposes.

Equally tragic was David's decision to seek a tryst with Bathsheba (2 Sam 11). However great his raw sensual desire that drew him to her, David also coveted in this case—a point that Nathan the prophet implied when confronting him about the incident (2 Sam 12:1-9). David thought he needed to be gratified through a provision that God intended for Uriah the Hittite alone.

Another grandiose misstep of David's was his decision to build a temple for God (2 Sam 7). David dearly desired to carry out this project, and spent considerable energy musing about it. Yet God explained to David that he didn't have the right temperament for the task, since he was a warrior at heart (1 Chron 28:3-7, 1 Chron 22:6-10). He should instead allow his son Solomon to do it, during the latter's reign.

David's motives were certainly more commendable here than when he took the census or yielded to temptation with Bathsheba. God, in fact, commended David for his desire to build the temple (2 Chron 6:7-9). Yet he may have been influenced by unhealthy motives as well. David had been mentored by the prophets Samuel and Nathan, and undoubtedly had frequent contact with other dynamic religious leaders whom he esteemed. He may have felt inferior to these people in certain ways. He may have desired to prove to himself and others that he also could make an important contribution to his nation's spiritual life. It wasn't enough merely to be a good political leader; he needed to accomplish something that would deeply influence his nation spiritually as well.

One thing is certain: David's desire to build the temple had become an *obsession*. His self-worth had become wrapped up in seeing it accomplished. "He swore an oath to the LORD, he made a vow to the Mighty One of Jacob: 'I will not enter my house or go to my bed, I will allow no sleep to my eyes or slumber to my eyelids, till I find a place for the LORD, a dwelling for the Mighty One of Jacob'" (Ps 132:1-5).

God certainly did David an enormous favor by relieving him of the burden of thinking that he had to build the temple. By revealing to him that the temple project wasn't his responsibility, God gave David a treasured insight into his calling as king. He assured him it was okay for him to be who he was, to focus on tasks that fit his gifts and personality, and to leave the other responsibilities for those more suited to handle them.

Acceptance Takes Courage

In the same way, God speaks to each of us, urging us to realize that he hasn't made a mistake fashioning us as he has. He wants us to take great encouragement in the unique potential he has given us personally, even to feel exhilarated about it.

He wants us to be good stewards of our potential, too, and to take the wisest possible steps to invest it for his glory and the benefit of others. To do this effectively, it's essential that we be optimistic and hopeful, and think big about our possibilities. From time to time, we will need to take a substantial step of faith with our life, to open ourselves more fully to the opportunities Christ has for us.

Again, the important thing is that such a step results from our best understanding of how God has molded our own life. The danger is always that we try to think *too* big, and embrace dreams that are out of line with who we are. It's our desire to look good to others that so often makes us vulnerable to such idealizing. Our craving to be appreciated, respected and loved drives us to strive for accomplishments we believe they'll admire. While we can never let go of this desire completely, we're far happier not letting it control our destiny. Our greatest joy is found in living out God's unique design for our life.

We shouldn't underestimate, however, how challenging it can be to say no to opportunities that appeal strongly to our desire to be esteemed by others, but run counter to what is right for us. Choosing God's best often means letting go of our need to be liked by others, to some extent—sometimes to the point of feeling like we're throwing caution to the winds.

My uncle Hunter Davidson was president of Chevy Chase Land Company for many years, until he retired in 1980, at 75. He brokered real estate and oversaw development in one of the most prestigious communities of suburban Washington, D.C. He had many friends and associates who lived in large, ornate homes, and he had strong incentive to do the same. Yet when he was 60, he and his wife chose to move from their 100 acre farm to a five-room bungalow on a small lot in Washington Grove—a onetime vacation community of eclectic homes in Gaithersburg, Maryland. Freed from many constraints of house and property, Hunter turned his attention to tennis and became a dedicated player. He continued playing avidly into his 80s, developing a near-professional skill.

Hunter's passionate devotion to the sport probably added years to his life, and it certainly added life to his years, for he remained in excellent health until he was 91.

Hunter's decision to move to Washington Grove was ingenious and bold, for he went against strong social incentives to choose a living situation uniquely right for him. And, far from hurting his professional life, the move enhanced it, for it made possible a lifestyle that improved his health, vitality and motivation for his work.

I'm not suggesting Hunter's step would be right for everyone or even most of us. Some people realize their potential more effectively through the benefits of a large home, and some use that setting for significant hospitality and ministry. Canadian physician and stress expert Peter G. Hanson observes that some retirees actually do better to move to a larger home than to downsize.[3] The bigger home provides them an outlet for their creative energy, contributing to a level of challenge that promotes health.

What housing arrangement is right for us personally is highly individual. We simply need to be careful not to let self-esteem needs override the question of what will best enhance our potential for Christ. Choosing a home is one of those decision areas where we're easily swayed too greatly by our concern for others' approval. It can take courage to act against this inclination in order to do what's right for us. The important thing is to know yourself well, then to draw on Christ's strength to choose what's in his best interests for your life.

Our View of God Makes the Difference

As I'm writing this, a letter arrives from a friend. In it Carol shares about her own struggle to break the habit of comparing herself with others. The challenge for her, she explains, is that, in her unguarded thinking, she imagines that God is comparing her unfavorably with others and expecting her to live up to their standards. In reality, she knows God to be profoundly different. She knows he loves her uniquely, has a distinctive plan for her life, and doesn't expect her to be anyone's clone. But she has to dwell upon this realization to be transformed by it.

Carol has put her finger on the heart of the problem for many serious Christians. It has to do with our view of God more than anything. We have a default impression of him—that he judges us in light of how well we live up to the lifestyle and accomplishments of other Christians we admire. Underneath, we know God isn't like this. We realize he has made uniquely, and that we best honor him by respecting our individuality. But this enlightened view of God doesn't come naturally. We have a *chronic* tendency to lose sight of it, for it runs contrary to much of what we've been taught.

We need a view of God that frees us from this tendency, and infuses us with courage to be the individual he has made us to be. For this to happen, we need to devote generous time to reflecting on God's distinctive love for us. We need to remind ourselves constantly that it is he who has given us our individuality, and that he takes it into account at all points in his plan for our life. This outlook on God will give us the heart to take the steps of faith so vital to realizing our potential for Christ. But it takes serious time reflecting on this picture of God for our attitude to substantially change.

In addition to focusing in this way on God's nature, we should—again—devote significant time to letting him direct our thinking. Investing such time can make a radical difference in our ability to recognize and carry out his will. Give Christ substantial opportunity to influence your life—both to shape your view of God and to direct your decisions.

Then take heart. He wants to shake the foundation of your life with opportunities that reflect his best intentions for you, with insight to recognize them, and courage to pursue them.

And there's nothing grandiose about saying that.

8

Turning the Page

Since my understanding of my gifts and aspirations is always evolving, mid-course corrections are sometimes essential. I'm happiest and most productive if I make these changes, even if they go against others' expectations, or against those I've long held for myself.

LIFE IS FAR FROM AN EXACT SCIENCE. Each of us, as we navigate much unmapped terrain en route to realizing our potential, make some good choices and some bad ones. And we make some that are right for us at one time but not another.

We invariably come to points where we realize that a situation or a goal we've chosen to pursue just isn't working for us. Sometimes we discover that a dream we've devoted ourselves to earnestly doesn't fit us nearly as well as we had hoped. Yet a big part of us resists letting go of it, because we've staked our identity in it so strongly.

Jason is a gifted high school history teacher, loved by students for his ability to make an often dry subject interesting. Yet for years he had pursued a legal career. Although Jason was a talented attorney, he wasn't out of law school long before he realized that his passion for law was far less than that of his associates.

By his early 30s, he'd determined his strongest gifts and interests lay in teaching, not in fighting legal battles. The fact that he'd long been fascinated with studying history led him to conclude he should teach it. And working with his church's youth ministry convinced him he would enjoy teaching high school students.

Deciding that he ought to become a teacher was one thing. Mustering the courage to leave the legal profession was quite another, and it took him three years to do it. Changing careers not only meant disappointing his parents—who had urged him to become an attorney and paid for all his higher education—but admitting to others and himself that he had spent years chasing a dream that wasn't right for him. It also meant financial sacrifice—trading a lavish salary for a modest one, and finding a way to fund further education. Jason worried, too, if he had the potential to be a good teacher, and whether he could find a position with a high school.

Today, his only regret is that he took so long to make this change. It has opened up a much more fulfilling career for him, and one that has proven to match his potential remarkably well.

Why Change Is Difficult

Like Jason, most of us take a circuitous route in finding our career niche; few of us get it right the first time. The changes in direction we make personally may be less dramatic than his—like switching college majors, or taking a new job within the same profession. Yet many of us make one or more major career changes during our lifetime. Our self-understanding is always developing. Add to this the extreme latitude of choice we face in America today, and we can easily be into our 30s, 40s or beyond, before we find the career that fits us best. Jason's experience is not at all unusual.

Change is the stuff of our lives in many other areas besides career and education. Few of us live out our life in the same town where we grew up, let alone the same home. Most of us make at least several moves—some of us more than we can count—to new homes or regions. We may change our church affiliation from time to time, and our membership in other organizations and clubs. We rethink our commitments in endless other areas—to leisure activities, to leadership roles, to people, to goals for personal growth, to our style of living.

Our most difficult turning points often involve relationships. Not many of us make the journey to marriage without going through at least several dating relationships, and a variety of hoped-for ones, where our expectations rise and fall. Most of us endure some painful experiences in romance, and have to make a number of new beginnings.

What every major life change we make has in common is that it always requires us to give up something in order to gain something. No matter how strongly we desire to make a certain change, we have to sacrifice certain benefits we've come to depend on and enjoy to do it, and often a dream we've cherished as well. Letting go of the past is usually the most difficult part of changing directions. Like Jason, we can get stuck there, and wait far longer than we should to move ahead.

There are several reasons we may fail to let go of situations or goals that aren't right for us, even when we have convincing evidence that we should. Being aware of these tendencies that can hold us back can help us to avoid them, and to act more decisively when it's time to turn the page.

• *Loss aversion.* Some people are highly unsettled by any experience of personal loss or failure. They abhor loss so greatly that they prefer to live in denial about unhealthy situations in their life, and will remain in them way beyond a reasonable point. To break away, they fear, would be admitting too blatantly to others and themselves that they've failed. This same mentality makes them subject to wishful thinking that these situations will improve.

This outlook is termed "loss aversion" in the financial world. Investment psychologist Dian Vujovich explains: "To understand loss aversion, consider this scenario: A friend owns shares of a stock or a fund that has fallen precipitously over a period of time. Rather than reevaluating whether the investment is still a smart one, your friend decides to buy more shares. As the price continues to slide, your friend decides to hold on to the shares even though all the signs say to sell. You ask yourself, Why won't he just get rid of that loser?"[1]

Part of what fuels loss aversion, Vujovich notes, is that we tend to value our losses in life more greatly than our gains. The grief we experience over a personal loss is typically greater than our joy over a success of equal measure. The result is that an investor with loss aversion tends not only to hold on to losing shares too long, but to sell winning shares too quickly.

We can be subject to loss aversion in any area of life. We may find it easier to stick with the unhealthy relationship than to break it off, less threatening to stay in the profession that doesn't match our potential than to start over in a new career. We dislike giving the impression that we've failed to anyone, including ourselves.

To move ourselves beyond loss aversion, it helps to understand that a number of losses are usually necessary to merit a success in any pursuit. Successful investors understand this principle well. Some investment strategies follow the principle that far more securities in a portfolio will post losses than gains; one may still come out ahead by keeping these losses as small as possible and the gains as substantial as possible.[2]

In the same way, our aim in life shouldn't be to insulate ourselves against all possibility of failure, but to keep the losses we do experience as small as possible. The real loss is when we hold on to a bad situation too long. "Cutting your losses" is a helpful concept in business, for it implies you're taking a positive step by putting a stop to an unprofitable venture. This is a good way to regard dropping any losing situation in our life. Thinking in terms of cutting our losses reminds us that we're gaining, not losing, by letting go of it.

In the same way, Jesus taught his disciples an extremely redemptive concept when he urged them to depart from towns where they weren't warmly received, shaking the dust off their feet as they left (Mt 10:14; Mk 6:11; Lk 9:5, 10:10-11; see Acts 13:51). He not only indicated it was normal and acceptable for them to experience some failures, even when they were following fully in his will, but he gave them a positive, assertive step to break the emotional inertia of losing situations.

Most important, he implied they would enjoy some rewarding successes if they pressed on (Lk 10:2-9). The key was to keep their losses as minimal as possible and their gains as significant as possible.

Jesus' teaching on shaking off the dust is good to keep in mind whenever we need to gain the courage to cut our losses in any area. Reflecting on it can help us find the heart to let go.

• *Being true to ourselves.* In some cases we've identified so strongly with a certain dream for so long that it has become part of the fabric of our personality. Even if we find that a new direction suits us better, the thought of letting go of our old dream feels like an act of treason against ourselves.

When a friend of mine was in his young 20s, his parents told him they would one day move from their plush suburban home, and allow him to purchase it for a minimal price. For many years Rob looked forward to the time when he could move his family there. It would mean a major increase in living space for them and a much quieter neighborhood.

Eventually, his priorities changed. He and his wife decided they preferred to move to a more modest home in the country, near recreational activities they enjoyed.

Not long after they made this decision, his parents announced they were ready for him to buy their home. "The hardest part," Rob confessed to me, "was admitting *to myself* that I no longer wanted to do this particular thing."

Rob fortunately had the maturity to abandon his dream of purchasing his folks' home, in spite of his mixed emotions. Some people in a similar situation, though, would feel compelled to stick with their original intention, out of concern with being true to themselves.

No matter how attracted we may be to a new dream, we may

still feel like we're forsaking an old friend by relinquishing our original one. We should recognize that it's normal and human to feel this way. We're actually going through a grieving process in this case. It may help us to take some time to mourn what we're leaving behind, and allow ourselves to face these feelings fully. There's no shame in doing so; it's part of the adjustment process often involved even in welcome change.

We may also need to redefine what it means to be true to ourselves. We should regard it as staying faithful to an *evolving* understanding God's will and our own potential, rather than a static one. As we make the changes this growing understanding requires, we'll probably feel less than authentic at times with new roles and identities we assume—simply because we aren't used to them yet. This doesn't mean we're selling ourselves short by moving forward. Change of any sort can feel unnatural at first. The key is to allow ourselves reasonable time to adjust, and in time we'll likely grow comfortable with our new situations.

God guides us not by revealing elaborate blueprints of his future intentions for our life, but by inching us forward step by step. We cannot be more true to ourselves than by committing ourselves fully to this process, and to all of the emotional adjustments involved.

• *The fear of hurting others.* Another concern we may have is that others will be hurt if we take a new step with our life. This fear can have some basis. Friends and family members who've grown accustomed to how we are now may feel threatened by our changing. If they've supported us and rooted for us as we've pursued our current dream, their pride may be hurt if we abandon it for a new one. A more serious problem is that they may lose important benefits they derive from their present relationship with us.

We can never know for certain, however, how someone will respond to a step we want to take until we carry it out. Nor can we foresee fully how it will affect them. Sometimes we're surprised.

During college, I dated a nursing student for a year and a half.

We enjoyed a strong supportive relationship, and talked seriously about getting married. Gradually, though, I began to realize that we weren't a good match for marriage, since our vocational goals didn't mesh well. My interest in continuing the relationship began to wane.

Yet for over a month I hesitated to tell her, fearing the news would be crushing to her. Finally, I brought myself to do it, nearly certain she would break down in tears.

She did break down. Not in tears but in laughter. She went on to tell me that her feelings about the relationship had been changing in exactly the same way, yet she'd been afraid of hurting me by admitting it. We parted amiably, and today both of us, happily married to others, remain good friends.

My experience brings out one of the most important principles of faith we can keep in mind in weighing a major change: *If God is influencing us to take a new direction with our life, he is influencing others about it as well.* He is changing others' thinking—preparing the way for us to move forward, and to benefit, not devastate, those in our path. While we have no guarantee that others will applaud what we're doing, we're likely to enjoy some encouraging surprises. And if God is leading us to make the change we're considering, we may trust that what is best for us will be best for others as well.

This isn't to minimize the pain often involved in ending a relationship. My experience in college was unusual, unquestionably; breaking off a relationship can be the most difficult step we ever have to take. Yet we can't second-guess how someone will respond when we share our feelings honestly with them. Nor can we predict how God will strengthen us to handle the challenge of communicating on this delicate level.

Beyond terminating a relationship, others have the potential to be hurt by any major change we make. The desire not to purposely hurt others, of course, is commendable, and a vital part of caring for them with the love of Christ. Yet we can become too concerned about unintentional hurt someone may experience when we follow through with what God wants us to do.

We should remind ourselves that God will be changing people's hearts as we move forward. Some whom we fear disappointing may respond quite differently than we imagine. Chances are good that, in the long run, they'll be grateful we've followed our star. In any case, we're not responsible for their feelings. We may trust that by faithfully carrying out what God wants us to do, we'll best enhance his providing for the needs of others—including those we're concerned about hurting.

• *The fear of failure.* While there are many fears that can discourage us from a new venture, the fear of failure is often our greatest deterrent. Some fear of failing is healthy, for it prods us to plan carefully. Yet an inordinate fear of failure will prevent us from pursuing dreams that are appropriate for us, including many that God will enable us to achieve.

As in dealing with loss aversion, part of the solution to overcoming an excessive fear of failure is to revise our thinking about failure itself. It's not the ultimate disaster to fail. With hindsight, we so often realize that certain setbacks helped pave the road to a cherished success. The important thing is to be willing to cut our losses if we do fail, and to be ready to do so. Simply knowing that we *can* cut our losses if we need to, helps to blunt our fear of failure and to give us the courage to risk.

It's just as important to remind ourselves that we may not fail. If Christ is leading me to take a certain step, I may trust that he'll work in countless ways to bring about his best. Whatever the outcome, I'll be better off going ahead. And I have strong reason to stay optimistic that I'll reach the goal I've set out to accomplish.

Scripture encourages us also to expect considerable comfort from God in the face of fear. It reminds us often that, as we seek his help, he calms our fears and inspires us with courage. "Do not be anxious about anything, but in every situation, by prayer and petition, with thanksgiving, present your requests to God. And the peace of God, which transcends all understanding, will guard your hearts and your minds in Christ Jesus" (Phil 4:6-7).

Yet it also warns us not to let fear rule our lives or keep us from realizing our potential for Christ. The tragic mistake of the servant in Jesus' parable who hid his talent, was that he gave in too greatly to the fear of calamity. "I was afraid," he confessed to his master (Mt 25:25).

Especially interesting is how often Scripture exhorts us simply not to be afraid. "Do not be anxious about anything." The implication is that as we take decisive action to move ahead in spite of fear, we'll not only experience God's blessings in many remarkable ways, but relief from our anxieties as well. We overcome fear most substantially not by reflecting but by *acting*.

If God is leading you to take a new direction with your life, ask him to give you courage to embrace life and move forward. Don't ignore your fears—in fact, face them carefully. But determine not to let them control you. Resolve to step out in faith and to operate in the realm of faith. By doing so, you'll find the strength to leave the past behind, and to open yourself fully to God's best for your future.

Another Concern

Of course, it takes courage as well to hold on to a long-time dream that has never changed, but hasn't materialized yet. This is the other side of the coin. While we'll likely face the need to revise certain dreams, and to reinvent ourselves accordingly, life usually brings also some late-blooming episodes with dreams that have long endured. Appreciating this reality helps us find the heart to try again, even at unlikely points. And it helps us to keep hope alive when a dream seems at a standstill.

The important thing is staying flexible—being ready to change direction if it's recommended, but just as ready to hold fast to a dream that continues to fit us, even though its time hasn't come yet. We'll look at this second dynamic in the next chapter.

9

The Joy of Late Blooming

Delays—even major ones—don't necessarily mean God is nixing my dream. To the contrary, they may be his means of ensuring greater joy and effectiveness for me once the dream is realized.

WHEN GEORGE MULLER WAS A YOUNG MAN, he had a dream—an earnest hope for his life and legacy. He wanted to become an evangelist, who would take the message of Christ to the world. After several unsuccessful attempts in his 20s to pursue this career, he concluded it wasn't in God's plans for him. He gave up.

Until age 67. At this unlikely point in life, his dream finally materialized. For the next 20 years—until he was 87—Muller traveled thousands of miles, carrying out numerous speaking missions, and becoming one of the 19th century's foremost Christian statesmen.

Muller's experience illustrates one of the most fascinating and encouraging aspects of God's providence that we encounter in our lifetime. It's the fact that certain dreams we assume have failed and been forever denied by God, do eventually succeed—but later in life than we expected. In some cases, the dream comes about *much* later than we thought possible.

The corollary is that waiting often proves to be well worth it. By taking a circuitous route to our dream, we're better prepared to enjoy its benefits—and really do enjoy them more than if we'd achieved our heart's desire quickly and easily.

Often, too, we're more effective in carrying out the responsibilities that the dream entails. This was clearly true in Muller's case. En route to realizing his dream of a speaking ministry, he spent several decades building orphanages for the urchins of England. He achieved broad recognition for this work and for his remarkable faith-based approach to life and ministry. Through it all, he gained a platform from which to speak that would have been absent if he had jumped into evangelistic ministry when young.

The Long and Winding Road

Muller's example, of course, is unusual, dramatic and noteworthy enough to make the history books. I'm not suggesting that most of us will experience a late success with such notoriety. Yet if we remain open to God's leading, and optimistic about his possibilities for us, most of us will enjoy certain delayed accomplishments that *to us* are dramatic—in light of the expectations we've held for our life.

These late-realized dreams may occur in a wide variety of areas:

• Many accomplish important career or educational goals later in life than they had hoped—but they do reach them. I think of a friend who worked as a computer specialist for many years, but longed to become a pastor. In his 50s, he finally began taking seminary classes and steps to qualify for service in his denomination. At 56, he received his first church assignment, and entered a rich new chapter in his life, of effective pastoral ministry.

Then there's a friend who taught high school science, but increasingly desired to become a physician. At age 40, she entered med school, then jumped the countless hoops necessary for certification. Now in her young 60s, she has served successfully and happily as a family physician for many years.

• The best openings for friendships and relationships may occur when we're well into our adult years. Some find an excellent opportunity for marriage late in life, even for the first time.

Last summer I officiated a wedding for two dear friends of mine, Randall and Alice. At 61, it was Alice's first marriage. If you knew her, you'd be puzzled why this beautiful, vivacious, gracious woman, who had long wanted to be married, hadn't found an opportunity long before this. Yet it shows, again, how God's timing works so differently for each of us.

• Creative, artistic and recreational accomplishments can occur at improbable points in life. Some even begin activities in their later years that usually benefit from an early start in life, and succeed impressively. My mom took up oil painting for the first time at 63. Over the next fifteen years she developed a significant talent for landscapes, winning a variety of awards in women's club competitions. I mentioned earlier my uncle, also, who began playing tennis in his 60s (at 65, actually), continuing earnestly into his 80s and achieving a high-level skill.

• Efforts we make to influence someone that seem to fizzle, sometimes do bear fruit over time, long after we've given up. A friend of mine found that letters she'd written over 20 years before to a friend about faith in Christ had finally been retrieved by that woman in a moment of need, and had sparked a spiritual turning point.

The Benefits of Delayed Dreams

It's important that each of us stays open to late blooming—whatever it may mean for us—in order to keep our hope strong and our minds alert to new opportunities. Yet staying as open as we should be is challenging. We're human, and most of us find that disappointment hits us hard. We tend to reason from the specific to the general, and assume that one or two setbacks in moving toward a dream mean failure forever.

In fact, failure often contributes to our future success, for we learn from mistakes and become more effective where we've failed. But success is only possible if we try again—which won't happen unless we're optimistic enough to believe God will enable us finally to succeed. Just how can we keep this hope alive?

One thing that helps greatly is to appreciate why God may postpone the fulfillment of a dream, and the benefits that may come from its delay. Some of these advantages may include—

• *Saving something for act three.* When we're young, we imagine we'd like to have all of life's treasures at our feet at once. As we grow older, we're grateful some of life's best adventures have been delayed. God graciously proportions his blessings throughout our lifetime.

• *Putting success in the right perspective.* Any success we enjoy has the potential of taking on too much importance for us. It can become the central focus of our life, stealing our affection from God. God delays in bringing certain dreams about, I'm certain, so that we can first deepen our faith in him and strengthen our relationship with Christ. When success finally comes, we're less likely to make it an idol, and are more inclined to appreciate it as God's gift, and handle it responsibly.

A related problem is that we may think of certain blessings of life—such as marriage or a golden job opportunity—as a panacea, solving all of our problems and bringing endless happiness. In reality, the improvements these benefits bring are typically more incremental than monumental. God wants us not only to put our expectations in proper perspective, but to learn to enjoy daily life in spite of many unfulfilled needs. The fuller our life is apart from a dream's being realized, the more likely we are to benefit from achieving it. Because we aren't banking on the dream solving all our problems, we're less likely to suffer a letdown when it doesn't deliver perfection, and are better able to enjoy its true benefits.

• *Handling the responsibilities of success.* Any dream that we realize brings new responsibilities for us to handle. While we might imagine we're fully able to take on these burdens now, God often does us a favor by giving us more time to get ready. One of the best ways we can invest our energy during a dream's delay is in preparing more fully for its eventual responsibilities.

• *Fitting our piece into the larger puzzle.* The most unfathomable aspect of God's providence is that he fits the details of our life into an infinitely bigger picture. He not only has our own needs in mind in a dream's timing, but those of countless others. And he integrates our circumstances into an endless variety of other situations.

The most encouraging part is that when a dream delays, we often that find circumstances are more favorable for it when it does transpire. We simply can't predict the direction circumstances will take in any matter related to our life. When a dream is slow to materialize, we should remind ourselves often that circumstances may actually fit it better at some later time. We do well to stay hopeful.

• *The growth of anticipation.* A friend once took me boat shopping with him. After we'd spent some time looking at different models, I asked him if he was ready to purchase one. "I don't actually intend to buy a boat," he confessed, "for then I wouldn't have this dream to look forward to."

My friend's somewhat tongue-in-cheek comment actually points to one of the most important keys to patience and contentment we can learn. Anticipation has value as an end in itself. There's great joy possible in the mood of anticipation; it's an extraordinary stimulant and motivator. If we can learn to enjoy the experience of anticipating, we'll have the most effective possible antidote to rushing a dream prematurely, or to losing heart if it delays. Patience is *natural* for us then.

If we can become comfortable with anticipation, then it can grow over time. The result is that we actually enjoy the fulfillment of a dream more when it delays than when it comes about quickly. It's one of M. Scott Peck's cardinal principles in *The Road Less Traveled*, in which he stresses the supreme value of delaying gratification.[1]

• *Divine compensation.* There's also a more mysterious, spiritual dynamic to the postponement of dreams that's hinted at occasionally in Scripture. God, in compensation for the waiting one endures, may increase the experience of joy in a dream's finally being realized. Isaiah 6:17 and Zechariah 9:12, for instance, speak of joy being doubled in return for a long-delayed blessing. To be sure, we'd be wrong to take such passages as guaranteeing God will operate this way in any particular case of our own. Yet they do give us a basis for hoping this will happen, and remind us that the delaying of a dream can mean greater eventual blessings.

A Dream Fulfilled—and Then Another

While focusing on the benefits of a dream's delay helps us to stay hopeful in the face of disappointment, we also benefit greatly from real-life examples. When we look for them, we find many—both from history and the lives of people we know—of those who realized major dreams at unlikely points. Such stories also permeate Scripture, and are one of the most inspiring themes of biblical history.

My favorite of these biblical examples is Zechariah's temple experience, described in Luke 1:5-25. Zechariah and his wife Elizabeth were the parents of John the Baptist. The account of their conceiving John in old age is well-known, and a staple of the Christmas story. The angel Gabriel appears to Zechariah in the temple and announces, "your prayer has been heard. Your wife Elizabeth will bear you a son, and you are to call him John" (v. 13). Even though Zechariah and Elizabeth are "both very old" (v. 7), Elizabeth soon becomes pregnant, and at full term gives birth to John.

While the fact of this miraculous birth is inspiring enough, there's more to this story than meets the eye. Zechariah was a priest, whose division of Abijah was on duty at the time Gabriel encountered him. Like other priestly divisions, Abijah served the temple only two weeks each year. Many of the priests lived away from Jerusalem, had secular jobs, and traveled to the holy city only by choice when their division was on call.

Each day one priest was chosen by lottery to enter the holy of holies and offer sacrifice. What's most significant is that a priest was only allowed this honor once in his lifetime, and many never enjoyed it at all. When Zechariah was chosen for temple service that morning, it was the prize of a lifetime. Here on this one day, late in life, he not only received the angel's promise of a child, but enjoyed the fulfillment of a major vocational dream as well.

What a Difference a Day Makes
One thing Zechariah's experience reminds us of is how remarkably our life can change in the space of a single day. Harvest experiences do occur for each of us from time to time, and sometimes—as in Zechariah's case—we're completely surprised by them. We do best to begin each day with high expectations for that day. While we shouldn't base our well-being on whether unusual blessings occur that day, a certain hope for them is healthy, for it makes us more alert to special opportunities God may suddenly present us.

Hope for the Future
Zechariah's experience, of course, not only inspires hope for the day, but hope for the future. His being chosen for the temple service brings out how long-term persistence toward a goal—and availability—often do pay off. Zechariah undoubtedly had been making the sojourn to Jerusalem for decades before this cherished opportunity finally opened up.

Then there is the revelation from the angel. Most interesting is that Gabriel says God's promise of a child is in response to Zechariah's prayer: "your prayer has been heard." Most likely Gabriel is referring to prayers Zechariah and Elizabeth had made for a child long before this, when she was in her childbearing years. This is one of Scripture's most graphic confirmations that past prayers are not forgotten by God. Time and energy we expend in praying do bring results—sometimes quickly, sometimes over time.

We shouldn't conclude from this incident that God will normally bend the rules of nature, and enable a woman past menopause to conceive, if one simply prays hard enough. God obviously can perform this miracle if he wishes. Yet the Bible gives only one other example of his doing so (Sarah's conception of Isaac), and so Scripture clearly isn't presenting this possibility as the norm.

What Zechariah's experience *does* show, unquestionably, is that prayer can radically affect our destiny. Unless we have a clear basis to know God has shut a certain door, we have reason to stay hopeful when we've prayed earnestly, that God will bring about a given dream. And if the dream doesn't work out, we can still be confident the prayers we've made will bring benefit in many other ways.

Keeping Our Own Hope Strong

Have you lost heart over a personal dream that hasn't been fulfilled? Yet to the best of your knowledge, does it fit your gifts and interests well? Is it a good match for your life as God has designed it? It may seem that pessimism about the future is your best defense against further disappointment. But keep in mind the benefits of hope, and the reasons for staying hopeful, that we've discussed. Be careful not to write history with a gloomy conclusion before it happens. Stay open to fresh opportunities to move toward your dream that God may make possible for you.

Ask him to give you the divine ability to live in two worlds at once—to stay hopeful about your future, but to be happy right now even with certain dreams unfulfilled. Through his grace, you can achieve this balance in your outlook, and it's a vital part of the attitude of faith.

Most of all, remember that whatever happens, Christ desires the best for you and is working out an ideal plan for your life. That alone is an incomparable reason for hope. Take confidence from knowing it. And may it give you the courage to dream big and take steps of faith.

Moving On

I hope that our discussion so far has helped you to better clarify important directions God wants you take with your life, and that you're experiencing greater passion for life itself. I hope, too, that you're feeling more comfortable with the dreaming process, and that at least one dream is emerging that truly fits you well, and makes your heart race. If not, don't panic; keep reading. The discussion that follows in the next two sections should strengthen your confidence that you *can* achieve your dreams—by clarifying how to set goals, how to seek help, and how to deal with fears of failure and success. That confidence in itself should inspire greater vision for your future, for it removes barriers of fear that hinder you from recognizing what you most want to do.

So let's move on now to look at how to set a goal effectively. No other step is more important in successfully achieving a dream.

III

Getting Your Life in Motion Toward Your Dream

10

Goals That Work

An effectively-set goal vastly increases my potential for success. Appreciating the benefits goals provide helps me find the incentive to set them and carry them out. Following certain time-proven strategies in setting them gives me an important extra edge as well.

IN MAY 1999, my mom came down with rheumatoid arthritis almost overnight, then was diagnosed with chronic leukemia. By July, this happily independent, gregarious 86-year-old, required round-the-clock nursing, and seldom ventured from her second-story bedroom.

The cost of full-time nursing was devastating. Mom also longed for more activity and contact with people, but her body would no longer cooperate.

Assisted living was the obvious answer. For months Evie and I dragged our feet, though, certain that mom wouldn't want to leave her beloved home of 44 years.

By January, we at least had reached one conclusion. An assisted living facility near our home was far and away the best option for her. We met with a director there. They could take mom eventually, she explained, but had a six-month waiting list, and then no guarantee of space.

Then something snapped inside us. Six months was too long to wait, given mom's personal and financial needs. We set a goal—to have her happily moved out of her home and into a better arrangement by the end of February. I stress *happily,* for we weren't going to force her, but would do whatever we could to encourage a welcome transition.

Almost immediately we recognized a solution we had missed before. To this point we'd assumed we had no space to host her in our home, even for a short time. Now it occurred to us that we could convert our upstairs family room into a temporary guest room, until her apartment was ready.

Option one.

Then dawned option two. It was far more preferable, but seemed highly improbable. *What if?* I wondered. *What if the door that seemed presently closed at the assisted living home had a crack?*

In that nothing-ventured, nothing-gained spirit that only a goal can inspire, I phoned the director, and explained to her that we really needed to move mom out of her home soon. Did they possibly have a way to accommodate her temporarily, until her own unit was available? I was stunned when she replied that she'd look into it.

Several days later, she phoned back to say they had a guest suite available that mom could rent for as long as necessary. And the charge for it was less than for permanent residency.

Now the job of convincing mom. We were equally stunned to find that she needed no persuading. She was ready to move, and eager for a new adventure.

On February 25, 2000, we moved her into this haven, where she lived very happily—soon in her own apartment—until her death in July 2003. The improvements to her social life, health and finances were remarkable.

What a Difference a Goal Makes

This surely isn't the most dramatic story you've heard about goal setting. Our situation wasn't desperate. It wouldn't have been a calamity if we'd had to wait six months or longer to move mom into assisted living. Still, we were faced with a situation that was far from desirable, and wanted a way to improve it. Once we set a goal, things changed quickly.

The goal substantially influenced how Evie and I thought about our predicament. Our minds started working. We saw possibilities we hadn't recognized before. It also gave me the resolve to broach an option with the director of the home that I wouldn't have considered raising otherwise. After all, if they had temporary housing, she surely would have said so during our long interview. Yet simply asking the question made all the difference.

I'm certain, too, that the sense of urgency I conveyed when I phoned her affected her response, and her decision to explore an option at her mammoth facility that she normally wouldn't have mentioned. Our goal influenced the outcome.

There's no question, either, that the excitement Evie and I felt about this sudden open door was contagious to mom. Had we been less focused, and less convinced, she would have been less certain about wanting to move.

This story demonstrates how goal setting can help us resolve moderately challenging problems—the type we often try to tackle head-first without first establishing a clear goal. The same dynamics that worked for Evie and me in this case will work for any of us in setting more far-reaching goals to achieve our major life dreams. Nothing helps us more to accomplish a dream than having well-conceived goals. A major dream may require us to set a variety of goals of different dimensions en route to reaching it. The good news is that any of us can greatly improve our ability to set goals effectively, and, with them in place, can radically increase our potential for reaching our dream.

The Power of Focused Intentions

Pick up any book on human potential, positive thinking or the secrets of success, and you'll likely find the author extolling the benefits of goal setting. You may well find the writer declaring that an effectively-set goal *guarantees* your success.

I'd caution that life offers no guarantees. Even our best-laid plans never assure any outcome beyond question. If you set out tomorrow at 11:00 a.m. to drive from Baltimore to Columbus, Ohio, determined to meet a friend for dinner at 6:00 p.m., there's no promise you'll make it. Your car may break down. You may have an accident. You may encounter weather problems or traffic delays. You may suffer a heart attack, and make it neither to Columbus nor back home.

Life offers no guarantees.

Still, it's likely you will make your goal. If your car is in good running order, you know the route and exercise reasonable prudence, the odds are overwhelming you'll reach Columbus by 6:00 p.m. You can tell your friend you'll meet her, and proceed with confidence that you'll keep your commitment.

A properly-set goal in any area assures your success with similar probability. Probability so high that you can go forward with the conviction that, Lord willing, you'll accomplish your objective. Such confidence isn't audacious or brazen, but simply respects how God has designed human life to function.

With a major, long-term goal, you'll probably make some adjustments in the deadline as you move along, to be sure. You'll modify some aspects of your goal as well. Still, the likelihood you'll achieve your *primary* objective is very high, providing you've carefully set your goal to begin with, and your passion for reaching it remains strong.

The parallel to a road trip is helpful from another angle. If you're like me, you enjoy driving. Sure, it takes effort and focused attention. Yet it's much less arduous, say, than laying cinder block or studying for a physics final. You may grow tired while driving, need to rest and regain your energy. Yet most of the time it's fun, and seems natural and effortless.

When you're living out a goal that's well conceived, and truly right for you, you feel much the same way. Far from requiring he-roic self-discipline, the goal taps your natural motivation, and moves you forward at a pace that works for you. You may get tired or encounter obstacles, just as you would on a road trip. Yet, overall, the process is enjoyable—in part because you're fueled by natural energy, in part because you're excited about your destination.

How Goals Help Us

Let's look more specifically at the benefits goals bring to our life. There are at least eight ways in which they help us achieve our objectives and dreams.

1. Goals break the inertia. Inertia is the single greatest barrier to our achieving a dream. A body at rest stays at rest. Yet a body in motion stays in motion—and so anything we can do to get our life moving toward a desired outcome is beneficial. Monumental chal-lenges, which seem beyond our capacity and strength, suddenly feel surprisingly manageable once we begin to tackle them. Goals break the inertia, by giving us the incentive to take that first step.

2. Goals give us occasions to rise to. Dale Carnegie observed that our most deep-seated human need is to be important. We each long to be doing notable things with our life, and we instinctively give the best of our time and attention to those tasks we consider most important. A goal lets us draw on this natural energy, by al-lowing us to determine in advance that a particular objective truly is worth our most earnest effort. Once we've established that fact, the goal gives us an occasion to aspire to, providing the most effec-tive possible motivation to keep us in motion.

3. Goals focus our thinking and energy. Nature abounds with energy sources of unspeakable potential that vastly increase their benefit when harnessed and focused in strategic ways. A gently flowing river, dammed and forced to flow through a small channel, produces a ferocious output, capable of turning the wheels of a power plant providing electricity to an entire city.

Goals have a similar effect on our mental energy, enabling us to accomplish exceedingly more than is possible without them. Most important, goals harness our subconscious energy. They serve our subconscious notice that specific problems need to be solved, and enlist the most creative partner in our mental process as an ally. Before we know it, insightful answers begin to emerge that we've never considered.

We see an enlightening example of how a goal can ignite creativity in a familiar Gospel incident. Four men have a goal—to bring a paralyzed friend to Jesus for healing (Mk 2:1-12). They carry him on a pallet to a house where he's teaching, only to find that they cannot move him through the huge, dense crowd overflowing the home. Rather than accept defeat, they look for a solution, finding an unlikely one. Instead of going through the crowd, they'll go above it! They climb to the roof, remove tiles over the section of the home where Jesus is speaking, then lower the pallet carrying their friend through that opening—compelling Jesus' attention.

Far from being offended by their aggressiveness, Jesus is impressed with their faith (v. 5). He forgives the man's sins, then heals his paralysis.

What's fascinating about this incident is that these men, in their mutual determination, conceived a solution to a problem that most would have considered unsolvable. Had they been less determined and focused, I doubt that their minds would have worked as well. Inertia would have prevailed. They would have settled for sitting placidly in the back of the crowd as spectators, failing to seize the golden opportunity before them. The fact that they had a clear agenda sparked their creativity, and inspired an ingenious solution to a difficult predicament.

Goals stimulate our own problem-solving skills in a similar fashion. They also heighten our alertness to opportunities we'd otherwise miss.

4. Goals inspire others to help us. We each have a natural instinct to be generous and helpful to others. A goal that we set for ourselves best allows us to appeal to this instinct in others, for it provides evidence to them that their effort to help us will be worthwhile. It also signals to them what sort of assistance we may need, and helps them recognize more readily how they can support us. Goals enable us to appeal to another instinct in others as well—the desire to root for someone who is making an honest effort to improve their life.

Setting a goal also helps us clarify in our own mind what sort of help we need to seek from others, and strengthens our courage to ask for it.

5. Goals open us more fully to God's help and provision. Well-set goals are an exercise in stewardship—stewardship of the life God has called us to live. It only makes sense that God will more likely extend his help to us when we're treating the life he has entrusted to us responsibly. The help God provides to those who set responsible goals seems to be part of his common grace; human potential writers, for instance, often speak of "synchronicity" or "serendipities" that occur when a goal has been set—fortuitous coincidences that help you realize your objective.

How much more should we expect special help from God when, as a follower of Christ, we have set a goal prayerfully, seeking his direction and provision. The goal also increases our alertness to windows of opportunity God may be opening.

6. Goals increase both our confidence and motivation to carry out all of the details necessary to achieve them. The best-set goal includes a clear plan of action, describing what work will be done when. Because we have such a blueprint in place, we're able to give our full attention to any of its details, knowing that the time and space is there to accomplish the other steps when necessary. We work more confidently on any segment of our plan, for we're not worrying that we're robbing time from more important tasks. We're also more likely to enjoy the less-scintillating steps necessary to achieve a dream, for we recognize how they are moving us toward an objective we dearly want to accomplish.

7. Goals give us a basis for measurable results. Our plan of action also enables us to better judge whether specific work we're doing is actually helping us accomplish our objective. We're better able to work smarter, and to take corrective action when needed.

8. Goals give us something to celebrate. Because a goal gives us a clearly defined target, we know when we've hit it. We now have something specific and meaningful to celebrate. This jubilant occasion is not only a tonic to us when it occurs, but another carrot-on-a-stick aspect of a goal, beckoning us to see it through to the finish.

Setting Goals Successfully

Appreciating the benefits goals provide helps us greatly to find the incentive to set them. How, then, do we do this effectively? Goal setting is more of an art than a science, to be sure. The process that most helps you may differ from what works for me. Each of us needs to experiment to find what steps benefit us most personally. Still, there are certain approaches to goal setting that universally help people turn dreams into reality. Here are ten of the most important principles to keep in mind.

1. Goals should be based on strong desire. The most common reason goals fail is because we don't desire their results strongly enough.

Let's say I set a goal to become an accomplished pianist in five years. I may establish it for a variety of reasons. At one extreme, I may be motivated by intense desire: I passionately wish to be musical, crave the thrill of performing, or long for certain social benefits this skill may open.

At the other extreme, I may take on this goal more out of obligation, or for any of the unhealthy reasons we noted in chapters 6 and 7. Perhaps I've long felt I have some potential to play piano, and that I owe it to myself to develop it. Or I may have some legitimate desire to be a pianist, yet underneath have a much greater yearning to become an actor. We set many goals primarily for the momentary relief of guilt that establishing them brings, but not because we earnestly long for their results.

We need to be thoroughly honest about our level of passion in considering a goal of this magnitude. If I strongly desire to become a competent pianist, chances are good I'll succeed. If I'm setting this goal mainly out of obligation, or as a substitute for a more burning creative desire, it's unlikely I'll stick with it past the fifth piano lesson.

Goals should spring as fully as possible from deep-seated natural motivation. Basing them on such desire isn't taking the course of least resistance, but is a matter of stewardship, for even the most intense motivation remains unproductive unless focused through a goal. If I need to set a goal for an outcome I'm less than exuberant about, I should first do what I can to boost my desire for that result. Apart from keen motivation, I shouldn't waste my time pursuing a goal. If the goal is required for reaching a major dream, then I should constantly bring to mind my exhilaration for the dream and remind myself how this goal fits into the bigger picture of my life.

2. Goals should be achievable. Goals should also fall clearly within our range of potential. Again, this isn't taking the course of least resistance, for goals stretch us to grow in ways that would never happen otherwise. Consider, too, that we each have vast possibilities for accomplishment within our areas of potential that will never be realized apart from concentrated effort. It only makes sense to choose our goals from this huge pool of options rather than from outside of it.

We should be confident also that we can relate temperamentally to the process necessary for achieving a goal. Not that we have to find all aspects of it scintillating. But if, for instance, I know that I'd find the regimen of practice necessary to become a competent pianist repugnant, I shouldn't lock in to this goal. *Some* enjoyment of the process in this case is important.

3. Goals should be specific. Goals should be clearly stated, both in terms of what we choose to accomplish, and the date when we plan to reach our target. Staying open-ended at either of these points greatly reduces the possibility that we'll achieve our objective.

4. Goals should involve a clearly-defined plan of action. One of the greatest benefits of goal setting is that it allows us to take charge of our life. We're able to peer into the future and lay claim to the time and process that will ensure our success. Even goals that seem impossible for us often can be achieved, if we allow enough time to reach them and plan our steps wisely.

It's unlikely we'll be able to predict every step required to accomplish a major goal in advance. Some of the details will only emerge as we move forward. Still, we should do our best to predict the most important steps, and then determine how and when we'll take them. The more fully we can develop a map for the journey ahead, the more likely we are to reach our destination.

The single most important part of this planning is to decide specifically when we'll invest the time needed for taking the different steps required for reaching our goal, so we can protect it as fully as possible. Start by determining, as best as you can, how much total time you'll need. Then consider when, in light of your energy and creative flow, are your *best* times for pursuing your objective— daily, weekly, monthly, yearly. Look also at what other commitments you'll need to rearrange or cancel to make way for this time. Design a schedule, even if it covers many years, which allows sufficient quality time for accomplishing your dream. Carving out this time, and guarding it as sacred, will make all the difference in hitting your target.

5. Goals should be established in prayer. While anyone can profit from goal setting, regardless of their spiritual orientation, we have an unparalleled advantage as Christians in planning our future. Through prayer we're able to connect directly with the heart of God, and enjoy the supreme benefits that result.

When setting a major goal, we do best to give some generous time to prayer. We should ask God to direct our thinking, to help us understand the desires and gifts he has given us that most deserve our attention, and to make the wisest choice of a goal among the many options before us. Just as important, we should ask him to give us courage to move forward with what he is prompting us to do. We should also ask him to help us determine a clear strategy for carrying out our goal.

Once our goal is established, we should commit it to Christ, in the spirit of Proverbs 16:3. Prayer, of course, should not end at this point. We should continue to seek God's direction and strength as we move ahead, asking him daily to show us any changes or mid-course corrections we need to make. It's here that goal setting can have the auxiliary benefit of deepening our relationship with Christ, by allowing us to experience his companionship in the great adventures of our life.

6. Goals should be flexible. Once we've established the process and deadline for achieving a goal, we should assume these details are realistic and follow them earnestly and confidently. Yet we should also recognize in humility that we don't know the future— how circumstances will unfold, or what doors God may open for us. Our understanding of our own potential is always evolving as well. There's no shame, as we move ahead, in changing the deadline for a goal, rethinking some of its specifics, or even dropping the goal itself if we find it no longer fits our life as we now understand it. Such revising goes with the territory, even in the most competent goal setting.

In 1997, my Christian band Sons of Thunder set a goal to produce a new album—our first in 25 years. Our plan was to accomplish this task with a $10,000 budget, three days of recording and three days of mixing, and to have a CD available by June 1998. The first shipment of CDs finally arrived on Christmas Eve of that year. By then, we had spent nearly $40,000, and made nearly 20 additional visits to the studio beyond what we'd planned. Still, there's not the slightest question that the album would still be a wish dream apart from our having had a firm goal, which galvanized these widely dispersed musicians and singers—spread out in eight cities around the United States—to accomplish a task we at first thought inconceivable.

The adjustments you have to make in pursuing a major goal may not be nearly as extreme as this. Still, you'll probably find it necessary, even with the best-laid plan, to make some revision in the timing and process as you move along. Yet you will hit your primary target, if you don't lose heart—and that's the important thing. And the fact that you have a goal will make all the difference in what you're able to accomplish.

7. Goals should be written down. Take time to record your goal and plan of action in writing. Articulate the details as precisely as you can. The process of writing helps greatly to clarify your thinking, and provides a reliable record when your memory lags. Apart from putting the specifics in writing, we limit the effectiveness of a goal—far more than we usually realize.

8. Goals should be rehearsed. We possess no ability—natural or learned—that doesn't atrophy when unused. Our ability to walk diminishes if we're bedridden only a short time. We should treat goals as we do our most cherished skills. We should "practice" them—that is, rehearse and reclaim them often. Most important, we need to rekindle our motivation for them frequently.

We should do this daily with a major goal. Take time to pray over such a goal each day. You may find it helpful to read over your written resolution, or recite it aloud. Visualize yourself succeeding. Imagine it's the day that you've finally achieved your goal; you're thinking back over all the time and effort you've invested to reach this point, immensely glad you never gave up. You're looking forward to a big celebration. Enjoy the exhilaration of this image for a moment. Then pray, asking God to help you make it a reality.

9. Goals should involve accountability and enlist cheerleaders. Most of us take great encouragement from knowing others are rooting for us to reach a goal. We benefit considerably from being accountable to others as well. Enlist your cheering squad—even if it's just one individual. Ask this person, or these people, to pray for you and encourage you as you work toward your goal, and make a pledge to them that you'll stay faithful to your intentions. Draw on their support as you move forward. And, of course, celebrate your victory with them when your mission is accomplished!

10. Goals should be celebrated! There's nothing unprofound in saying that we should celebrate a goal once we've reached it. In our driven nature, we can easily bypass time devoted purely to enjoying our achievement, out of zeal to move on to new projects. In devising a plan of action for a goal, we ought to plan in time for celebrating—not only our final victory, but also intermediate triumphs along the way. Knowing these occasions for rejoicing are in place will increase our incentive to move toward our goal. They will also give us special opportunity to thank God for what he has enabled us to accomplish—and, most important, to *feel* thankful to him, and to grasp in our heart as fully as possible all that he has done for us.

Goal setting should add a substantial element of joy to our life, for we're taking action to improve our life, and to harness our creative potential much more constructively. The hope for this joy is an important incentive to move forward.

Experiencing this joy is also critical, for it deepens our gratitude to God, enhances our health, and boosts our productivity and the benefit of our life to others. Planning times simply to experience such elation isn't frivolous, but part of the process that will best enable our life to be a channel of God's grace to the world.

Reaping the Benefits

Goal setting, more than any other factor, holds the key to achieving our important dreams. Appreciating this point is extraordinarily encouraging, for it means recognizing that God has given us much greater control over our destiny than we normally suppose.

If you have a dream that isn't moving forward well, let me encourage you to break it down into manageable goals. Give *serious* time to doing this, even if it takes many hours or days. Make it your initial goal to come up with a set of achievable goals that will move you successfully to your dream. Devote yourself earnestly to the process of setting them, and stay with that process until these goals are firmly established.

Then set out on the journey of accomplishing them one by one, keeping your eventual goal of reaching your dream firmly in mind. You'll likely revise your goals and their deadlines at many points as you move ahead. But the important thing is that your life is now in motion. You're giving God much greater freedom to direct and redirect you as well. With this map in place, you're far more likely to reach your destination.

11

Cheerleaders and Mentors

I will derive unspeakable benefit from exposing myself as fully as possible to people who view life positively and my own life dynamically.

FOR SOME TIME I'D BEEN STRUGGLING to ride a two-wheel bike without training wheels, but with no success. I kept repeating the same ritual—peddling a few yards until the bicycle began to tilt, then putting my foot out to break the fall. My problem wasn't inability but lack of confidence. A bike has to be moving at more than a snail's pace to stay upright. But I was frightened to peddle fast enough to give it the needed thrust, afraid I'd wipe out severely.

My dad was convinced I would learn to balance, and kept reassuring me. His confidence gave me the hope to try and try again. With his help, I was able to enjoy the fantasy of conquering the two-wheeler for brief periods of time. Dad would hold on to the bike's seat and run alongside while I peddled furiously. We'd make good headway for a block or two until he got winded. I was adamant about one thing, though: he wasn't to take his hand off the seat. I kept reminding him again and again.

One day he decided to trust his own judgment. After ambling

through several hilly blocks, we came to a level stretch entering a new development next to our neighborhood. I began peddling hard and picked up a head of steam. The momentum felt great, and I turned my head to smile at dad. Only then did I realize that he hadn't been holding the bike at all, but was standing with arms folded a block back, grinning from ear to ear. I had accomplished my first solo bike ride without knowing it!

My victory with the two-wheeler came for a single reason: my father believed in me more than I believed in myself. He kept encouraging me to try, then took his hand off the bike at just the right moment, so I'd discover for myself that I could do it. He believed in me to the point that I succeeded.

It was one of those landmark childhood experiences that I now look back upon as a parable to my life, for it reflects something I've often experienced. At important turning points there have been those who, like my dad with the bike, have seen my potential better than I have. Their confidence, encouragement and wise counsel have inspired me to move ahead. It's humbling to realize how dependent I've been upon their help.

I suspect you'll say the same about your own experience. When we think carefully over our life, we usually find the same pattern: God has used people with high expectations of us to prod us forward at many critical times. Their help has been vital whenever we've been able to reach a personal goal or take an important step of growth.

It's a near-necessity for most of us when we embark on a major dream or goal to have those special friends who believe in us, and help us find the heart to press on. We'll probably need those who advise or coach us as well. And depending on the nature of any goal we set, we may need a more formal program of training or education to get us from here to there. But that program is simply an organized means of drawing on the help of *people* in accomplishing our goal, and if we're fortunate, people who are positive about us and see our possibilities.

Those of us who are more independent in nature may underestimate our need for others' encouragement and help. So I want to look now at our substantial need for cheerleaders and mentors in what we accomplish, and to encourage you to seek the support you need. More than anything, we benefit from simply being around people who see us dynamically and believe in our potential—sometimes more greatly than we ourselves do. This is the lesson I learned so dramatically when trying to master the two-wheeler.

The Substantial Impact of Others' Expectations

Like it or not, others' expectations affect us, and do so dramatically. Countless studies in the social sciences demonstrate the point. Too often the effect is negative. Others may have no vision for us at all. Or they may form a static impression of us that doesn't change—the familiarity problem that Jesus encountered in his hometown of Nazareth (Mk 6:1-6).

The effect of others' static expectations can be stifling. A friend in her forties told me that her parents still think of her as sixteen. "And when I'm with them, that's exactly how I act," she said. The default mode for each of us is to rise or fall to the expectations others have for us. Even Jesus, in taking on our humanness, allowed himself to be influenced by others' expectations. Mark notes bluntly that when Jesus returned to Nazareth after beginning his public ministry, "He could not do any miracles there" (Mk 6:5).

Even when others have high expectations of us, these may be based on their own ideals or ego needs and have nothing to do with our actual potential or God's intentions for our life. How many parents push a child to succeed in some area foreign to the child's aspirations or gifts.

Yet God also brings into our life people with high expectations of us that are based on a realistic understanding of our potential. They resonate with our personal dreams and have the grace and wisdom to help us realize them. These are the blessed souls who see our life dynamically. Such people are incomparable gifts of God to us, peerless friends who help us experience his best.

People who see us dynamically benefit us in three important ways. One is through their optimism. We each are far more suggestible than we normally assume. We're affected greatly by the attitudes of those around us, and are especially prone to absorb others' attitudes *about us*. Yet if pessimism is contagious, optimism is as well. Another's confidence that we can succeed soothes our insecurities and helps us gain the courage we need to take bold steps.

Those who see us dynamically are also often the ones best equipped to help us with their counsel. Because they see our potential better than we do, they may see the steps we should take to realize it more clearly as well. Not all positive thinkers in our lives are wise counselors, to be sure. But those who are able to inspire us by both their optimism *and* their counsel provide us an immeasurable service.

In addition, those with high expectations of us who are in a position to do so (parents, spouses, coaches, teachers, close friends) often find creative ways to nudge us into taking challenging steps. From the parent who takes his hand off the bike at just the right moment, to the high school coach who risks putting us fourth in the batting lineup, to the friend who sets up a blind date for us with the one we marry—supportive people find inventive ways to help us realize our dreams, and provide us with important occasions to rise to.

Facing Our Need for Supportive People
Again, though, many of us underestimate, often greatly, our need for supportive people. We may assume that, as Christians, we should learn to depend solely upon God at all times and never count upon others' help. The rugged individualism of our American culture, too, drives us to think that we're more mature if we can solve our problems, resolve our decisions, and accomplish our goals with as little help from others as possible.

Scripture does teach that God often helps us directly, apart from anyone's assistance. Yet it never encourages us to *presume* upon this happening. Here God takes us through an interesting odyssey in the Christian life. On the one hand, he wants to teach us that he is all-sufficient to meet our needs. From time to time, he puts us through experiences to teach us that we can draw our strength from him alone, and shouldn't lean unfairly on other people. Yet he also wants us to understand that he has made us social creatures, and that he frequently uses others to provide us with encouragement, motivation, direction and support. As soon as we learn the first lesson, it seems, it's time to learn the second!

When Moses began leading Israel, he first had to learn the lesson about depending upon God alone. God needed to wean Moses of an unhealthy dependence upon Aaron as his personal spokesman.

But in Exodus 18, we find the situation has changed radically. Moses isn't depending *enough* upon the help of other people. The Israelites are well into their journey through the desert, and Moses is booked to the teeth with responsibility. On a typical day he "took his seat to serve as judge for the people, and they stood around him from morning till evening" (Ex 18:13).

Moses' father-in-law, Jethro, comes to visit him then. Shocked at how overextended Moses has become, Jethro admonishes, "What you are doing is not good. You and these people who come to you will only wear yourselves out. The work is too heavy for you; you cannot handle it alone" (Ex 18:17-18). He urges Moses to share his responsibilities with capable leaders from among the people, and suggests a process for doing so.

Moses follows Jethro's advice and delegates many tasks. The steps he took to share responsibility probably added years to his life, and certainly increased the quality of his life and leadership in many ways.

The passage teaches us two lessons about our need for others' help. One is the importance of letting others share our burdens, and of drawing on their help in many areas. The other is our need for the *enlightenment* God provides through other people. What I find most striking about the incident is this: Moses communicated with God more closely and directly than anyone in the Old Testament (Ex 33:11, Deut 34:10). God often gave Moses explicit guidance, and even revealed to him in exacting detail the directions for building a sanctuary in the desert. Yet God didn't give Moses any direct guidance about how to manage his time and priorities, or about the need for delegating responsibility. It was left to a trusted friend, Jethro, to offer this critical advice.

We learn that vital insight and inspiration needed to realize our potential may not come directly from God, but from supportive, dynamic-thinking people whom he inspires to help us. If we don't open ourselves to their help, we're likely to live beneath our potential. And we may fail to enjoy some of the most welcome provision God has for our needs.

Finding People Who See Us Dynamically

Realizing how much we benefit from the influence of such people should come as welcome news. It means we each have a means available that can help us better realize our potential, accomplish our goals, and experience God's best. Yet this news may be unsettling as well, especially if we feel that our options for finding supportive people aren't good. Those of us who've grown up in unaffirming families may feel we're at a particular disadvantage and that we've lost a step in life.

Scripture, though, is full of examples of people from difficult family backgrounds who went on to live rich and fruitful lives. David, one of the most impressive heroes in Scripture, is an inspiring example. His father Jesse thought so little of him that he didn't invite him to participate when Samuel interviewed his sons for the position of king (1 Sam 16:1-13). David's oldest brother, Eliab, apparently despised him, for he chided him for thinking he could confront Goliath (1 Sam 17:28), and his other brothers may have disdained him too. Yet God used all of this adversity to toughen up David for super-human tasks.

It's clear that David also succeeded in overcoming the effects of an unsupportive family by seeking affirming relationships outside of it. His friendship with Jonathan is a prime example.

Our need at every point in life, with every challenge we face, is to "play the hand we're dealt." Where others' support is lacking, God makes make up for the deficit in many ways. Yet each of us also has among our acquaintances and potential contacts far more opportunities for supportive relationships than we normally imagine. Here are some suggestions for finding supportive people:

• *Begin with prayer.* Our need for supportive, dynamic-thinking people is so close to the heart of God's concern for our life that it's clearly an appropriate topic for prayer. Pray regularly that God will bring you into contact with those who believe in you, and who inspire you to realize God's best for your life. Mention this concern daily in your devotional time, and from time to time pray about it more extensively.

If your need for affirming relationships is significant, don't hesitate to take an afternoon, a day or longer for a personal retreat to express your need to God. Be sure to thank him for the supportive relationships he has provided you in the past. Ask him, also, to help you understand any changes you can make that will better help you find these relationships in the future. Then move forward in light of the insights you've gained.

• *Take inventory of your relationships.* Carefully think over your friendships, family contacts and other acquaintances. Is there someone you know who by instinct thinks positively about you, gives you good counsel, and inspires you to meet challenges? Is this person open to a closer friendship? If so, you may want to give more time to nurturing this friendship and drawing on this person's strength. As much as possible, give priority in your social life to those who see you dynamically.

By the same token, if some acquaintances are outrightly unaffirming and belittle your dreams, avoid contact with them as much as possible. Take control of the time you spend with people, and maximize that spent with those who encourage you.

• *Teachers and coaches.* I'm often fascinated at the bond that can develop between us and a teacher or coach, especially one who's training us in a talent we're eager to develop. I've seen so many cases where a teacher has seen a student's potential far better than the student has, and by optimism and skillful instruction has inspired the student to heights he or she never thought possible. Often the side effect is that the student grows more optimistic about life in general.

A dynamic bond can sometimes develop in a short period with a teacher we've never previously met. It happened the first night for my son Ben, in sixth grade, with a most unlikely candidate—a 74-year-old hearing-impaired drum teacher with several disabled, arthritic fingers. On Thursday nights for the next five years, Johnny Smith, a retired Washington, D.C. jazz drummer, worked magic with Ben. In a tiny, makeshift basement studio, Smith taught with the aid of only several cheap drum pads, a few homemade wooden cymbals, and an ancient hi-fi system with distorted speakers. He not only taught Ben invaluable techniques but, most important, constantly assured him that he could master the drums, and praised each small step forward. Smith's impact was such that Ben was a highly-skilled drummer by high school. He then majored in music and percussion in college, and today teaches high school band.

The magic, though, can occur for us at any age. I mentioned earlier my mom's late-blooming success with landscape painting. It started when, at 63, she took a painting course at a local women's club. Her teacher recognized a latent talent and encouraged her to take painting seriously. For many years, she studied under this gifted instructor, who inspired her on with his confidence.

I don't mean to imply that anyone can count on becoming the next Buddy Rich or Grandma Moses just by sitting under the right teacher. Each of us, though, does have areas where we're far more capable of blossoming under a qualified instructor than we typically think. If you have a skill you're eager to develop, pray earnestly, ask around, and see if you can find a gifted teacher who will work with you. Then take the risk—sign up with him or her for a course or private lessons. Give the teaching process a fair chance, and see how it goes. In some cases, the impact of an inspired teacher can be thoroughly life-changing.

• *The healing help of counselors.* Professional counselors, by their training and often their temperament, naturally focus on seeing people dynamically. Counselors can benefit us in a variety of ways—from clarifying our thinking in decisions, to helping us better communicate, to helping us resolve deep-rooted conflicts. The right counselor can do us a world of good.

In most metropolitan areas, you'll also find many Christian counselors, some on church staffs, who are qualified to help with your area of need, while respecting your values and commitment to Christ.

There are also many counselors today who focus not on conflict resolution, but on training clients to live successfully and accomplish their goals. Often called "life coaches," you'll find them in metropolitan areas and sometimes on large church's staffs. Good life coaches by their nature are possibility thinkers who see your potential well. The right life coach can aid you tremendously in achieving a goal, both through helping you map out strategy and by being a supportive friend.

If you believe you can benefit from professional counseling or life coaching, don't hesitate to seek such help. Counselors do differ greatly in their approaches, and you may find more rapport with one than another. Feel free to interview several in seeking the one who's right for you. For some of us, counseling or coaching can fill a substantial void, and provide exactly the missing support we need toward reaching a goal.

• *The benefits of an active social life.* Any steps you take to become more socially active increase your chance of making friends and meeting affirming people. Joining a social club, of course, can do it. There are endless other possibilities, though. Taking a course at a community college, or through your county's adult education program, may yield a friendship with the teacher or others in the class. You may likewise forge lasting friendships by joining an athletic team, or a music or drama group. Or by volunteering with a community organization or mission that can use your talent. There are vast differences in the social climate of different groups—in the supportive spirit present, the chemistry you may experience with the members, and the likelihood of finding friendship. It can take some research and experimenting to find the settings that work best for you.

It can happen, too, that you become stigmatized unfairly in any social situation, or discover that its climate is by nature unsupportive. You may be surprised, though, to find how radically differently people treat you in another setting—even a similar group in the same community. The experience of changing social situations can be as extreme as moving from one country to another.

I offer suggestions for finding social opportunities and awakening your social life in *Overcoming Shyness* (chapters 9-12)[1]. As a rule, the more active you are socially, the greater your prospects for meeting supportive people and forming affirming relationships.

Gaining even just one friend who believes in you proves a matchless treasure when you take on a goal. God often uses such a friend to help you chart your course. And your friend's positive expectations and hope for your success will help you find the heart to stay *on* course toward your objective.

• *The golden opportunities within Christian fellowship.* Some of the most affirming people on this planet are Christians who've been deeply touched by the grace of God. Compassionate Christians with a dynamic, grace-centered perspective on the Christian life are often extraordinary encouragers. I visit few churches and fellowship groups where I don't encounter at least some of these notable people. And some Christian communities, because of the focus of their teaching and ministry, tend especially to attract them.

Our primary motive for joining a church or Christian group, to be sure, should be to grow in Christ. Yet it's also important to be looking to the Christian community as a source for supportive relationships. I don't mean to overlook the complexity often involved in deciding which church or fellowship group to attend, and when it might be right to leave one for another; I look at some of the issues involved in these choices in *The Yes Anxiety* (chapter 13).[2] But the good news is that most of us have many excellent options for Christian fellowship available within the region where we live. Often these include many opportunities we haven't yet discovered. Over time, we'll likely find that the Christian community provides us with the best setting for forming special friendships with supportive people.

• *See others dynamically.* Finally, in looking for supportive relationships, it's hard to overstress the importance of "doing unto others." If we're eager to find those who are affirming and forward-looking with us, one of the most important steps we can take is to act this way toward other people. Encouragers attract encouragers. Fortunately, there's much we can do to improve our social skills and sharpen our ability to see others dynamically.

One of the most endearing qualities of Jesus during his earthly ministry was his uncanny ability to see people dynamically. Consider his remarkable encounter with the woman at the well in Samaria (John 4). He was able to see beyond her erratic past and recognize her possibilities. The impact of a few minutes interacting with Jesus was so profound that she went on to become the most effective witness in the Gospels, drawing hoards of Samaritans into contact with Jesus.

May this incident inspire us to see others' possibilities, and to encourage them in the ways we hope to be encouraged ourselves.

In the same way, may it inspire us to look for dynamic-thinking people to support us as we move toward our goals. Whatever the goal or dream you've embraced, there are people out there who can help you achieve it, by believing in you, encouraging and coaching you. Think of these folks as God's special agents—for indeed, that's what they are.

12

Finding the Heart to Ask for Help

I may benefit another as greatly by asking for that person's help as he benefits me. If God intends me to receive someone's assistance, then he is preparing her also to respond to me positively. Appreciating these dynamics helps me find the courage to seek the help I need.

I WANT TO DEVOTE A BIT MORE ATTENTION to the challenge we often face in asking for others' help. It's easy enough to say we need others' support in pursuing a dream or goal. But we may feel less than comfortable asking for it. And, of course, we need others' aid to achieve our objectives in many ways beyond basic support and coaching. But the thought of asking for certain types of help (employment, financial assistance, connections) may seem mortifying.

Why is asking for help often so difficult?

Shyness is a common reason, and for the many of us who are shy, it doesn't take much to pull us outside our comfort zone. If we're seriously shy, just asking someone to pray for our success can feel like we're asking for their heirloom.

Yet pride can be the culprit as well, even if we're not shy at all. We may regard asking for help as a sign of weakness, and prefer attempting a task by ourselves that can be accomplished much easier and more effectively with others' assistance.

Overcoming shyness and swallowing pride go with the territory for many of us in pursuing a major dream. While we need to work at conquering these inhibitions, nothing helps us more in a given case than simply strong desire. When our passion for a dream or goal is great enough, we're more naturally able to push beyond our reluctance to seek assistance. So doing whatever you can to stoke your desire for success helps tremendously. When it's strong enough, it trumps both fear and pride.

Praying earnestly for God's help helps greatly also. Ask God to make your dream's desire intense enough that you'll find the heart to seek the help you need. Scripture shows constantly that God emboldens us in response to such praying—it works!

Still, there's another factor that can keep us from asking for help, even when neither shyness nor pride holds us back. It's the fear that we'll impose on others. Those of us who are highly empathetic by nature, especially, may worry we'll inconvenience or annoy others by asking their aid. We may even convince ourselves it would be unchristian to do so.

This fear is occasionally justified. But it's so often not that we ought to assume it's illusory, if we're waxing overanxious about burdening others. Here, remembering our past experiences that showed this concern baseless can help.

Let me share with you one of my own, which taught me dramatically how this fear is sometimes 180 degrees from the truth. It also taught me volumes about God and his willingness to provide for us through others' assistance.

Help from an Unlikely Source

It was a late summer evening, and Nate asked if he could spend the night with a friend who lived about a half hour from our home. I agreed to drive my fourteen-year-old son there.

After dropping him off, I drove only a short distance away when my Ford van's engine sputtered, then shut off. I couldn't restart it, so I let the car drift to a stop at the bottom of hill, then trudged back to the house to phone for help.

I reached Evie at home, who agreed to come for me. But after I gave her copious directions to this remote country home, she suddenly gasped and said there was a small problem: she had no car available. Ben, our other teenage son, had borrowed hers that evening, since his was disabled.

Evie said to sit tight while she tried to locate Ben on our other phone. She returned a few minutes later to say that none of Ben's friends knew where he was. There was good news however: The father of one of his friends had volunteered to come for me.

While I was relieved to know help was on the way, I was embarrassed to be inconveniencing this neighbor, since I barely knew him and it was already past 11:00 p.m. I also knew this had been a terribly difficult year for Jim, for his seven-year-old son had died of a heart problem that past fall. I felt bad troubling this man or his family in any way.

Yet Evie said Jim was already on his way, and so I had no choice but to accept the favor. I walked out to the street to wait for him. A fog had settled in so thick that I couldn't see the house from the road, and I worried that Jim wouldn't be able to find his way there. I feared also that by now he was feeling dumped on and regretting he'd offered to help.

When Jim finally arrived, shortly before midnight, he threw his car's passenger door open and greeted me with a warm handshake and friendly smile. I thanked him earnestly and apologized profusely for inconveniencing him. He insisted he was happy to help, and his demeanor conveyed it.

Jim drove me to my car, and I was surprised to find I could start it now. He agreed to follow me as I drove home. We found our way to the country highway back to Damascus. Unfortunately, my engine was starting to lose power again. Soon it died altogether, and I was stuck now on the shoulder of Route 27.

Jim offered his car phone so I could call for road service. This was no small favor, for it was 1994, and the cost of operating a mobile phone was still outlandish. Finding a tow truck this late at night took a while, and I had plenty of time to chat with Jim. I learned that this man, whom I knew only as a quiet neighbor, was president of a large Washington association and travels constantly. Finding that he had to arise early for a one-hour commute, though, did little to lessen my embarrassment over taking him from his home at this hour.

A tow truck finally arrived at 1:00 a.m. Jim and I followed as it hauled my lame van to the repair shop we frequent in Damascus. When the driver wouldn't accept a credit card, Jim handed me $50 in cash to pay him. Jim then drove me home. He seemed as cheerful and alert when he let me off as when he had picked me up, and showed no hint of resentment that my misfortune had just robbed him of several hours sleep.

Helping Healed the Helper
It wasn't until I dropped by his home the next evening to give him a gift and thank him, that I learned the full reason for his happy benevolence that previous night. Earlier that evening, he explained, he and his wife had gone for a walk in their neighborhood. Their carefree spirit was fractured when a neighbor asked how they were faring in the wake of their son's death. A sentimental discussion followed, and they all reminisced over how much they missed the boy.

"I came home feeling sorry for myself," Jim said, "and convinced life had dealt me a dirty blow. I lost my bearings for a while. It was while I was wallowing in discouragement that your wife phoned. For some reason, hearing that you needed help broke the spell. And I actually felt like my son was telling me, 'Go ahead and help him.'"

Now I don't believe that deceased persons communicate with the living, and I don't think Jim meant that he literally heard his boy's voice (those who are grieving often use such language). I'm inclined to think God was prompting Jim, in a way that Jim interpreted through his own filter.

What did become clear as Jim talked further was that Evie's call had had a surprisingly healing effect on him. He didn't want to be feeling sorry for himself, yet was stuck in the inertia of self-pity. Finding he could do something constructive to help someone else allowed him to redirect his energy positively—a striking paradigm shift. Driving around some fog-drenched country roads and losing a few hours sleep was a small tradeoff for regaining his sense of purpose and optimism.

While I feared we'd inconvenienced Jim greatly, we in fact had done just the opposite. Evie and I unknowingly had helped him by letting him know of our need for help.

The Challenge of Asking for Help

It was an experience I'll never forget. At that moment my car died, I felt helpless. I wondered if I could find my way in the fog back to the home. When Evie informed me she was carless, I felt the bottom had fallen out of everything. Little did I realize God had not only prepared someone to bail me out, but that helping me would be hugely beneficial to him.

The incident is such a wonderful parable to our broader life's journey. We need others' support in so many ways in carrying out our major dreams and goals. But our fear of imposing on people can keep us from asking for their help, *and* may deprive them of blessings in the process.

This isn't to deny that we can lean too heavily on others' good will. I recall a man who once arrived in Washington, D.C., in a ramshackle automobile with condemning Bible verses painted on all sides. For the next year or so, he lived out of this car, parking in church lots and streets of northwest Washington. He depended on the charity of Christians to provide money and food for him and his several dogs, who slept in the car with him. He declared unabashedly that his life's mission was to help Christians learn to be more generous, by giving them the opportunity to serve him.

Well . . .

His example is extreme. Yet it does bring to mind how one's dependence on other people can become unhealthy—in his case dysfunctional. Banking on others' help can become an unwholesome habit, a problem Paul addresses in 2 Thessalonians 3:6-10.

For serious Christians, though, the problem is more typically the opposite. We feel uncomfortable asking for others' assistance, and so often out of fear we're inconveniencing them and not being properly self-reliant. We should keep two factors in mind, though. One is that the same God who is working within us is working in others' hearts as well. When God moves us to take a step of faith, he prepares others to help us along the way. Where he wills our success, he inspires others to take an interest in our needs.

The second point is that, more often than we think, we do others a service by allowing them to help us. The opportunity to assist us may meet important emotional or creative needs for someone. It may give that person a needed sense of being useful, or a chance for new experience and growth.

Others are often far more eager to be of help than we assume. In some cases the opportunity can be life-transforming. This was clearly so with Zacchaeus, a revenue official who encountered Jesus in a crowd in Jericho (Lk 19:1-10). As a despised chief tax collector, he had surely lived self-indulgently to this point. Yet his attitude changed suddenly when Jesus looked up at him, at his observation post in a sycamore tree, and declared, "Zacchaeus, come down immediately. I must stay at your house today." Not only was Zacchaeus thrilled to host Jesus, but the opportunity awakened a compassionate side in him that undoubtedly had long been repressed. "Look, Lord!" he announced. "Here and now I give half of my possessions to the poor, and if I have cheated anybody out of anything, I will pay back four times the amount."

Most interesting is how assertively Jesus conveys his need for help. Hosting Jesus in this case was no small task. It probably involved several meals, and some of Jesus' disciples likely accompanied him on the visit. Most of us would feel awkward even asking a friend to consider inviting us for dinner. Jesus was comfortable *telling* Zacchaeus that he and his party were coming over for food and lodging. Jesus was able to speak so straightforwardly to Zacchaeus because he knew he wasn't imposing on him, but doing him a great favor by giving him this chance to serve.

For Zacchaeus, the change in outlook was astounding. In an instant, the pleasure of acquiring was transformed into the joy of giving. It is one of the Bible's most profound descriptions of a paradigm shift.

The message is not that we should pick up our phone and announce to our neighbor that we'll be dropping by for Sunday brunch. Yet Jesus' frankness in sharing his need with Zacchaeus does help free us from our fear of imposing on others. We're reminded that asking for help can sometimes be a genuinely compassionate move!

Facing the Challenge

The point has especially strong bearing for our major steps of faith. In pursuing an important dream, we invariably have to ask help from people in a variety of positions, including some we may consider too important to approach. One of the most gratifying discoveries we can make is that those in the most prestigious posts are often there because their desire to be helpful is greater than normal. By asking their assistance, we're tapping into natural energy that's part of their personality. Far from imposing on them, we're encouraging them, by giving them a chance to extend themselves in yet a new direction. We benefit greatly from their help, and they benefit also by providing it.

We're especially likely to experience this synergy when we're praying for God's direction and timing about whom to approach. Asking help from "important" people gives us one of the most remarkable opportunities we ever experience to stretch our faith and experience the faithfulness of God. Understanding this dynamic of human nature—that many truly enjoy extending help—helps us find the courage to seek it.

Of course, it's true that some we beseech are annoyed by our asking and may not even bother to respond. We still benefit then, though. We grow through the experience of asking, and discover we're able to handle any rejection involved and move on. We learn an important lesson about our resilience. We're also able to check off a possible source of help from our list—clearing our mind to look for someone better suited to assist us.

The important thing is to keep in mind this broader principle of life—that some are willing to help us and even are genuinely pleased to do so. In each case, we need to keep asking till we find that individual whose heart God has touched to help us.

Are you stuck in moving toward a dream—knowing you need others' help but fearing you'll impose on them too greatly by asking? Remember that if God has inspired your dream, he's inspiring others to support you. Realize, too, that he may want you to grow through the experience of asking for help. So put that process in motion. Pray earnestly, then consider your options. As God leads, and scary as it seems, ask others for the help you need. Then keep asking, till you find the right people to assist you. Take on this venture in faith, even if it feels like you're living on the edge. Don't short-circuit the provision Christ has for you—or the adventures he has in store for you!

13

Prayer and Your Personal Dreams

God limits some of his most important provision for my needs to what I choose to request through prayer. Because of this, I should pray earnestly and often for his help when pursuing a major dream.

IT'S INSPIRING ENOUGH that Jesus performed his first miracle at a wedding. The fact that he changed water to wine at a wedding feast in Cana, as his first extraordinary act, symbolizes his abundant willingness to bless all the particulars of bringing two people together in marriage. It reminds us, too, of the miracles he can work in the process.

Yet there's another dimension to this event that's equally encouraging to consider. Jesus performed this miracle *in response to someone's request.* Apart from the earnest urging of Jesus' mother, the six earthen jars would likely have remained so many empty vessels.

So it is with most of Jesus' feats recorded in the Gospels. He performed the vast majority in response to someone's plea for assistance. As such, they give us not only a message about Christ's power, but also about the significance of prayer. In the case of his healing miracles, he never turned down a single request for help. Jesus solved an immense problem for each person he healed. Yet I'm touched just as deeply with how the person's courage to ask for help played an important role.

I'm always moved profoundly by biblical examples of answered prayer. Among my favorite are passages that speak of God granting petitions for a child. "And the LORD remembered her; and in due time Hannah conceived and bore a son, and she called his name Samuel, for she said, 'I have asked him of the LORD'" (1 Sam 1:19-20 RSV). And, "Do not be afraid, Zechariah, for your prayer is heard, and your wife Elizabeth will bear you a son, and you shall call his name John" (Lk 1:13 RSV). I'm often stunned to think that God allows us to influence our destiny, not only through our actions but our petitions.

Appreciating how broadly and emphatically Scripture shows prayer to be effective, should encourage us to make bold requests about our personal needs. Saying we're mandated to do so is not putting it too strongly. In reality, though, many Christians feel squeamish giving much attention to personal requests. They fear such praying is selfish and a diversion from more reverent concerns.

We can overdo praying for personal needs, unquestionably. Yet some attention to it is essential. It's especially important if we have a major dream that's propelling our life. We need to be seeking God's direction, and his help and success at many points also—with both our broad dreams and our specific goals. Let's look at how such petitioning should fit in to a healthy prayer life.

The Three Purposes of Prayer

Scripture speaks of three broad roles that prayer should play in our lives. The first is its effect upon our attitude—its redemptive influence on our own disposition and outlook. Through prayer our attitude becomes more Christlike; we become more inclined to do God's will, and we grow more encouraged as well. There are a variety of approaches to prayer that point us in this direction, from confession, to praise and thanksgiving, to meditation, to praying for the grace and strength to accept God's will—as Jesus did in Gethsemane.

The second role of prayer is its effect upon our understanding. By praying for God's direction, and through silent, prayerful meditation, we position ourselves for God to influence our thinking, and we vastly improve our grasp of his guidance. It's through such praying that we're able to establish which dreams and goals reflect God's best intentions for our life.

These first two roles have to do with prayer's effect *upon us*. Yet just as frequently, Scripture reminds us of the influence prayer has, not only upon us, but *upon God*. While the Bible never implies we can manipulate God through prayer, it does emphasize that God purposely chooses to limit much of what he does in our experience to what we choose to pray for. He graciously extends to us the possibility of having influence through our petitions. This third role of prayer is as critical to healthy spirituality and to living effectively for Christ as the first two.

This third role cannot function effectively without the first two. Our single greatest need as Christians is to stay in a relationship of trust with Christ where he can encourage and guide us. The first role of prayer most clearly nurtures this relationship. The benefits of a renewed heart extend to all areas of our life—inspiring health and vitality, the ability to enjoy our present situation, and the capacity to think clearly about steps of faith we should take. Through praying specifically for God's guidance (prayer's second role), we sharpen that understanding further, and our sense of intimacy with Christ benefits immensely.

The benefits of prayer's third role, though—both in strengthening our relationship with Christ and enabling us to live effectively for him—shouldn't be minimized. By making requests of God, we grow through taking responsibility. We also gain a valued sense of partnership in what he is doing. In his extensive study of prayer in Scripture, John Calvin concluded, "We see that to us nothing is promised to be expected from the Lord, which we are not also bidden to ask of him in prayers."[1]

Scripture consistently shows, too, that the possibility of having influence through prayer is much greater than we normally think. The biblical emphasis of this point is so pervasive that it led African pastor Andrew Murray to declare, "As image-bearer and representative of God on earth, redeemed man has by his prayers to determine the history of this earth."[2]

Practicing the Privilege

When it comes to praying for a major personal need or dream, no one would deny the importance of prayer's first two roles, in keeping us grounded and encouraged in Christ and alert to his direction. We clearly do well to give ourselves to this whole realm of prayer Scripture recommends. But what about the third role? How important is it to ask God pointedly to meet a need or to make a dream or goal possible? I find that Christians generally have two hesitations here.

One is the fear that God doesn't want us to spend our energy praying over such self-focused matters. Don't we do best to devote the petitioning part of our prayer life to more ministry-centered concerns?

There's no question that we need to pray faithfully for others' needs and the broader concerns of Christ's ministry. Yet Jesus told us also to pray for our "daily bread," implying we should give at least some attention each day to raising our personal needs to God. Paul made basically the same point in Philippians 4:6, when he declared, "Do not be anxious about anything, but in everything, by prayer and petition, with thanksgiving, present your requests to God." God, then, has encouraged us to be straightforward in bringing our personal needs before him.

More troubling for many, though, is the question of how bold and persistent we should be in raising a personal concern to God. What if you've done so for months, years—or decades!—without receiving an answer? Doesn't the point come when you should cease your petitioning and simply pray for acceptance?

The answer of Scripture is surprising. Jesus encouraged his followers to continue bringing requests to God until they received a clear answer. To this end, he told two parables—one of a widow who continued to implore a judge to vindicate her case in court (Lk 18:1-8), another of a man who continued to ask a friend for bread to serve to an unexpected guest (Lk 11:5-8).

At first this emphasis on importunity seems brazen and irreverent, tantamount to pestering God. Yet, in reality, some vital benefits come through long-term persistence in prayer. One is that our desires become clarified. When we persist in making a prayer over a period of time, we give God the fullest opportunity to work within us—either to change our desire or to deepen our conviction that we really do want what we're asking.

In addition, persistence may be needed for the deepening of our faith. When we've prayed only briefly about a matter, we're likely to think an outcome has resulted from our own effort or fortunate circumstances. Long-term persistence in prayer deepens our conviction that we truly need God's help and that he is behind the solutions that come.

It's striking that in both of the parables Jesus told, someone persisted in asking help for a rather limited personal need. Certainly in a matter as life-changing and far-reaching as a major personal dream, we should assume God not only permits us to continuing praying for its success but wants us to do so.

Abusing the Privilege

This isn't to say that praying for a personal concern can't become obsessive. It does so if it either robs us of our well-being in Christ or diverts our attention from other responsibilities in prayer. A Christian woman in her mid-thirties, who told me she was continually depressed over being unmarried, also admitted, "I spend a lot of time walking around my yard getting angry with God over my predicament." While I respected her honesty with God, I feared her prayer life was doing more to hurt than help her. In this case, the third role of prayer was far overshadowing the first two. Her ongoing argument with God about wanting marriage simply nurtured her frustration over being single. It did little to strengthen her contentment in Christ or to help her gain perspective.

A friend of mine and his wife had a similar experience, in praying about their infertility. He told me, "We made this a matter of constant prayer over a long period of time. After a while, we discovered that our prayer life was little more than an attempt to try to jerk God's chain in order to get a child. Sure, our prayer life included adoration and intercession on behalf of others, but it was just preliminary measures to get to the real issue. Finally, we realized that daily, persistent prayer for a child was not only damaging the other aspects of our prayer life, but was also causing us to focus on this one matter in our daily activities. Our lives became consumed by this one issue."

Interestingly, they decided to stop praying for a child on a consistent basis. He notes that "after we made this decision, I was able to focus more on communicating with God and growing in my spiritual walk with him. When my prayer life changed, I actually believe God gave me more insight into how I should approach the infertility crisis. I truly felt a wisdom from God about life in general that I'd not experienced earlier. My decision-making ability was greatly improved. And only then were we able to make some responsible decisions about our crisis."

My friend's experience brings us back to what the primary purpose of praying should be—an activity that helps us gain a joyful, Christ-centered perspective on our life. If you find your prayers for a personal need are doing the opposite, you should look carefully at why this is happening. It's possible you'll do best to stop praying for this matter altogether, at least for a time.

More probably, some adjustments in your prayer routine will solve the problem. Try giving at least half your time in regular devotions to praise, thanksgiving and devotional practices that strengthen your joy in Christ. Then, in the time you spend making requests, give most of your attention to other concerns besides your personal one. Spend significant time praying for the needs of others. Limit the time praying for your personal matter to two or three minutes at most. That should be adequate time to express your concern, without letting it become the main focus of your prayer life.

Of course, there may be exceptions to this pattern. If you're facing a major decision regarding an important personal dream, then you may need to give more attention to this area for a time. But as a general rule, it's best to be persistent yet succinct in bringing regular petitions before God. Remember that most prayers of petition in Scripture are brief and to the point. And many were far-reaching in their consequences.

Extended Prayer—a Special Privilege

There's also, though, an important place in Scripture for special times set aside for praying for special needs. Jesus in Gethsemane, Hannah in the sanctuary, Moses in the wilderness, and many other examples, remind us of the benefits that come from extended praying about a pressing need. Such occasions can yield invaluable insight into new directions for our life. They can also provide outstanding opportunities to pray for God's help with dreams and goals already in place.

The desire for marriage, for instance, often justifies a personal retreat devoted to praying about this concern. To be honest, I seldom find that someone who wants to be married has ever spent an extended time praying for this need. My impression is that most Christians don't take this level of praying as seriously as they should.

My experience gives me reason to be optimistic about the benefits of such extended prayer. When I was 26, I spent a day on a personal retreat for the purpose of asking God to provide me a wife. The event is vivid in my memory, for I picked a striking and beautiful setting for this prayer time—the Blue Ridge Parkway and Skyline Drive route through central Virginia, as I drove home to Maryland from Roanoke.

It was about six months afterward that my relationship with Evie began to develop, leading to our marrying a year later. I suppose I'll only know in eternity if there was a relationship between that day spent in prayer and God's bountiful provision for my need. However, I suspect the connection was more than coincidental.

Whether it's marriage, or any other dream you have that doesn't seem to be moving forward, extended prayer can help remarkably. If you've never done so before, let me recommend setting aside a generous portion of time—an afternoon, a full day, a weekend perhaps—for the purpose of praying to God about your need. It's certainly not asking too much to give a day or two to an effort that may have lasting benefits. At the very least, you'll grow closer to Christ through the time. And it may open you more fully to his provision.

Remember that such a time shouldn't only allow you to express your desires to God, but should give him room to do his redemptive work within you. Be sure to plan your personal retreat with a view toward both of these goals. Devote time to thanking God for how he has provided for you in the past. Pray for acceptance of your present situation. Allow liberal time, too, for silent reflection. This is an opportunity for God to bring order to your thoughts, and to help you see steps you may need to take to find an answer to your need.

But don't feel squeamish about clearly expressing your dream to God. Ask him to change your heart if, in fact, this aspiration isn't right for you. Yet be straightforward also in asking him to help you achieve your dream, within his own wisdom and timing. You won't force him to do anything he wouldn't otherwise wish to do (Rom 8:26). But through this process you'll give him greater freedom to bring about his best for your life.

Whether in these special times of prayer or daily devotions, we should take heart that God wants us to bring our petitions boldly before him. The biblical message on this point could hardly be clearer. Before you make the effort to pursue a major dream or to find the answer to a pressing need, give some serious attention to praying for Christ's direction and help. This can make all the difference.

14

Meeting the Optimism Challenge

The despair I'm feeling over a setback is an instinctive response that may bear little relation to reality. I need to understand my temperament well, and counteract unhealthy reactions.

WHEN THE STOCK MARKET CRASHED in October 1987, Jake feared it meant the end of life as he knew it. He had pinned his financial hopes for retirement upon years of careful investing in securities.

Within a day, chest pains landed him in the hospital. The diagnosis: a heart attack. His body had caved in to the bad news along with his emotions.

Jake did recover, and, after a long hospital stay, returned home and lived another eight years. The stock market gradually recovered as well, and Jake's holdings never plunged into the freefall he feared. Yet market ups and downs constantly unsettled him. He worried often that he hadn't set aside enough for retirement, and that a downturn would spell financial ruin for him and his wife.

Ironically, after he died at 83, his widow found that Jake's portfolio totaled over $700,000. He, unfortunately, had no orderly method for tracking its value, and most of his numerous stock and bond certificates were stuffed in a safe deposit drawer. He was thus left to ruminate about their actual worth, and often imagined the worst. In fact, he had more than enough to live comfortably, and about half his holdings were bonds, which don't typically lose their value during stock market declines.

A friend of his confided in me, "I just don't believe Jake had any idea how much he really had."

From this one picture of Jake, you might conclude he was simply a pessimist—unable by nature to see the glass half-full in his financial world. In fact, this Boston attorney would better be described as an optimist and positive thinker in most ways. Yet he could grow despondent under certain conditions, and was particularly vulnerable with his finances.

Facing Our Own Potential for Despair

While we have to navigate many situations en route to achieving a dream, often our greatest challenge is simply managing our own temperament. Our prospects for success may be outstanding. But ultimately, all we have to go on is our perceptions, which can be skewed greatly. If we perceive our options as poor, or regard a setback as fatal, our assumption will become a self-fulfilling prophecy.

If I'm going to accomplish a major dream, it's vital I become good not only at thinking strategically, but psychologically. I need to strive to understand myself, and how I instinctively react to both success and disappointment. It's important, especially, to be keenly aware of how I respond to setbacks. Do I take them in stride? Or do I tend to reason outward from them, and assume a single misfortune spells doom for my whole endeavor? We need to recognize how susceptible we are to despair when problems occur, so we can counteract that slide if it sets in.

Jake's experience with the stock market shows how even a basically optimistic person may despair under certain circumstances. It prods us each to look carefully at how we may be similarly inclined, and at how we can avoid such a plunge into clouded thinking.

Each of us has what psychologist Robert Bramson terms a potential for despair, which can be set in motion by various factors. Yet we seldom recognize this tendency as a personality trait, let alone an unhealthy reaction. The result is that we normally don't think of it as something we can modify or control. Rather, we consider ourselves victims of despair when it occurs.

Yet despair by its very nature is almost always an overreaction, often severely so. We assume we're doomed to failure in a situation where we may still have plenty of reason for hope. Even worse, we may conclude from one setback that we're snakebitten, and that the bottom is falling out everywhere else in our life.

The potential for despair we each experience is also a uniquely personal one. What triggers despair varies greatly from person to person, and often has to do with our past. If we've been seriously slammed in some way, or know others who've been, we may inordinately fear the worst recurring in that area. We're shell-shocked, and it may take little to convince us that life is turning against us there.

Jake, born in 1912, was in his late teens and 20s when the Great Depression settled in. It broadsided for him what are usually one's most optimistic years. Seeing once-high-riding executives selling apples on Boston streets indelibly impressed him that financial catastrophe does occur, sometimes to the least expecting. Those years programmed him to fear the worst whenever stock market indications soured.

If we've likewise suffered a major tragedy or setback in our effort to reach a cherished goal, we may be predisposed to expect defeat if we try further. Even when our prospects are good, we perceive small setbacks as calamitous, a single failure proving the doors are forever bolted shut.

The Inertia Factor

The most unfortunate part of despair is that it's an emotion with inertia. Left unchecked, it takes on a life of its own. A case in point is the lame man in John 5, who lay by the pool of Bethesda. He staked his hope for healing upon a popular belief—that when the pool rippled, an angel was present, and the first person into the water would be healed.

Yet he also regarded his situation as hopeless. "I have no man to put me into the pool when the water is troubled, and while I am going another steps down before me," he explained to Jesus. What's most stunning is that this man seemed to regard his dilemma as permanent; he had been ill for 38 years and "had been lying there a long time."

Jesus challenged his gloomy thinking, asking him, "Do you want to be healed?" By posing this question, Jesus suggested this man's attitude was working against his getting well. Yet he also implied that the man could break the inertia of his despair, and take steps toward healing.

The incident is a good one to keep in mind when we're facing a situation we think is hopeless. It challenges us to stop and consider whether our outlook itself is preventing us from seeing a solution. We're reminded that God gives us greater control to remedy the predicaments in our life than we tend to think. And Christ is on our side as we make the effort to see things more optimistically.

Winning the Fight
Fortunately, there's much we can do to stop our tumble into despair when it occurs, and to prevent it setting in, in the first place.

I'm not blandly suggesting the Christian never suffers defeat, nor has reason to feel discouraged. We suffer losses at times so severe that grief is the most appropriate reaction. Grief is healthy then, up to a point, and part of the healing process through which we come to terms with our loss.

But too often despair, as in Jake's case, is an extreme reaction, triggered more by the fear of calamity than the reality. And even when grief is appropriate, in response to a genuine loss, it can linger too long, and blind us to new beginnings and reasons for hope God provides us.

Here are some steps that can help us break the spell of unhealthy despair.

• **Know yourself.** Understanding our own psychology, and what makes us vulnerable to despair, helps us recognize how to avoid it.

Learn to identify despair as soon as it starts to set in, and to realize you're giving in to a deceptive emotion. Remember how your past predictions of doom have usually been wrong, and recall specific instances. Realize that your present fears are likely unreasonable as well, and take comfort in that. If you possibly can, laugh at your tendency to catastrophize, which is only too human.

Think over your life, and recall instances when you've given in to despair. Identify the circumstances where you're vulnerable. If you know that certain situations tend to trigger despair, you can be braced for that happening when you have to face them. Being clearly aware what these circumstances are also allows you to choose to avoid them, if possible.

• **Withhold judgment.** Steve Simms, author of *Mindrobics: How to Be Happy the Rest of Your Life,*[1] offers this advice for when life fails our expectations: *withhold judgment.* Take a deep breath. While he excepts obvious tragedies (a loved one's death, for instance), he insists we're usually on good ground not to negatively judge situations that disappoint us.

Simm's advice is sound wisdom. Most of our negative judgments are based on scant information; we don't know what's happening behind the scenes, nor how events will continue to unfold. Over time, we often find that setbacks have benefited us surprisingly. With the advantage of hindsight, we see them in a very different light. Given that, we do well, as a matter of principle, to resist judging them negatively, at least until sufficient time has passed.

• **Take inventory.** It's also very helpful simply to think as clearly and broadly as we can, both about the situation depressing us and our life in general. Despair results because we focus too much on one area—usually a setback or defeat we've suffered—to the exclusion of everything else.

Jake would have benefited from having an accounting system that allowed him to easily calculate his net worth. Merely being able to inventory his holdings would have let him see that his financial picture wasn't as bleak as he imagined. In the same way, taking inventory of a situation we're distressed about—looking at as many aspects as we can—often helps us see it more hopefully. In addition, we benefit from prodding our focus beyond this one problem to the other options we have, and the fuller picture of what God is doing in our life.

Most of us can use assistance in taking such inventory. Having a friend or counselor who views us positively, and is gifted in helping us see our life's bigger picture, helps immensely. We derive great benefit, too, from times of prayerful reflection, where we allow the Lord an unhindered opportunity to influence our thinking.

• *Shake off the dust.* But what about the more fundamental question of whether we should simply avoid certain circumstances? If we know a specific situation triggers our capacity for despair, should we try to stay clear of it altogether?

The answer depends upon God's purpose for us in the situation. Is it likely to help or hinder us in realizing our potential for Christ?

It is, of course, a prevailing theme of Scripture that God often is concerned not with changing the situation, but changing us. He brings many difficult circumstances into our life to help us grow. His concern is that we learn to handle challenges effectively and not be easily unsettled by adversity (Jas 1:2-4).

Yet, as we've stressed, Scripture also has plenty to say about being good stewards of our life, and about managing it in ways that make us most productive for Christ. This means at times responsibly deciding to leave a situation where we find it hard to be productive. One of the factors we must weigh is how we relate to the situation emotionally.

Again, it helps to remember that Jesus exhorted his disciples to leave towns that ungraciously received them, and to shake the dust off their feet as a testimony against the people (Mt 10:14, Mk 6:11, Lk 9:5, 10:11; see Acts 13:51). We might have expected him to encourage his disciples to be long-suffering then—to bear joyfully with those treating them poorly, and wait patiently for them to change. Yet he clearly intended his disciples to stay productive. I suspect, too, that he didn't want them to bog down emotionally in the inertia of unfruitful situations. He wanted them to stay as optimistic as possible about evangelizing, for in that spirit they'd most effectively minister.

The New Testament's most dramatic example of shaking off the dust is Paul's decision to switch his focus from the Jews to the Gentiles (Acts 18:6). Paul was extraordinarily attached to the Jews, and highly susceptible to discouragement when his efforts to convert them failed. He went so far as to write, "I speak the truth in Christ . . . I have great sorrow and unceasing anguish in my heart. For I could wish that I myself were cursed and cut off from Christ for the sake of my brothers, those of my own race, the people of Israel" (Rom 9:1-4). I suspect that part of God's purpose in shifting Paul to the Gentiles was to allow him to work in a more optimistic climate. While the Gentiles still offered him many challenges, he was more naturally resilient with them.

From Paul's example, and similar ones in Scripture, we can take heart that it's sometimes okay to leave or avoid a draining situation. The important question is how it contributes to realizing our potential in the long run. We ought to base our major commitments, as much as possible, upon how well an option fits our personality and gifts—including our natural ability to cope. By choosing major situations that match our temperament (career, job, church, relationships, hobbies, etc.), we're simply being good stewards. Yet we'll need to adjust to many challenges within each of these settings, in order to reap its long-term benefits.

Jane, for example, is a highly-skilled journalist who loves writing more than any other field. Yet she takes even moderate editorial criticism hard, and rejection of a piece she's written crushes her. Jane shouldn't avoid a journalistic career because she's prone to these reactions, but should strive to modify them. Here, a counselor or support group can assist her invaluably in learning to take critiquing less personally.

At the same time, Jane should feel free to leave an unaffirming job for a more affirming one. Choosing one where people are supportive of her and her work, or leaving one where they're not, is simply exercising good stewardship.

• *Limit contact with negative people.* One point is abundantly clear from all of us: we should feel great freedom to limit our contact with highly negative people. Yes, Christ calls us to love and minister to those who are difficult to love, unquestionably. Yet he never expects us to be a doormat to anyone. If someone purposely is constantly insensitive or abusive to us, we shouldn't feel obliged to maintain any friendship with that person at all.

Many difficult people, to be sure, aren't intentionally unkind, and may even have their compassionate side. Still, their view of life is dour. We may feel that Christian love demands we spend time with them, for the sake of our positive influence. Yet we need to be honest about their influence upon us as well. If we find we're easily dragged into their pit of despair, we shouldn't place unrealistic burdens on ourselves. We may do best to limit our time with them to small doses, and to balance it by spending generous time with people who are positive about life—and about us.

• *Strengthen your trust in Christ.* Recently a friend invited me to visit an Alcoholics Anonymous meeting she regularly attends. It was my first chance to witness in person this program I've long admired from a distance.

Although I was familiar with AA proceedings and thought I knew what to expect, I was stunned by the humility these people displayed. Person after person spoke candidly about being powerless to remedy their problems apart from God's help.

The experience impressed me with how beneficial it is to face problems we have that are chronic. Yet how seldom we do. As Christians, we're chronically inclined to lose the perspective of faith on our life. Yet usually we fail to appreciate just how recurrent the problem is.

Simply facing how perpetually our faith needs rekindling, is our single most important step toward keeping our heart encouraged in Christ. Nothing fights our slide into despair more effectively than grasping how fully he can be trusted—both with our present and our future. Yet we need to remind ourselves of this *constantly*, for faith that seems so vibrant one day eludes us the next.

The great news is that, as we make this effort to refocus our attention on Christ, he always responds with what John calls "grace upon grace" (Jn 1:16 RSV)—that is, an endless supply of grace for our needs.

While our capacity for despair is considerable, our capacity for faith is even greater. As we move toward the dreams God has placed in our heart, we should make every effort to keep our faith strong. In that spirit, we'll be able to put setbacks in perspective, and keep our long-term vision strong. Here is the most important antidote to despair, and the greatest assurance that we'll stay open to the support and direction Christ wants to give us.

* * * * * * * *

It's hard to overstress the importance of striving to understand our own psychological makeup, and especially our personal "potential for despair." Recognizing those factors that trigger gloomy thinking, and being ready to counteract them, can make a huge difference in what we accomplish. Indeed, learning to manage our own temperament is as important as any other step we take toward achieving a personal dream.

It helps us to also think as broadly and creatively as we can about any setback we experience. Is there possibly a silver lining in it that we're missing? Does it possibly even imply that success is close at hand? Let's turn to that question now, and consider how to view setbacks in the most positive possible light.

15

Responding to Setbacks

*The setback I've encountered is a God-given opportunity
to learn, grow and become more successful; it may even
indicate that success is just around the corner.*

JACK CANFIELD IS EDITOR of *Chicken Soup for the Soul: 101
Stories to Open the Heart and Rekindle the Spirit.* Published in
1993, it has inspired over 200 spin-off titles, with more than 112
million copies and 40 translations in print.

Yet Canfield was turned down by 133 publishers before finding
one willing to take a chance with his idea.

Jack Canfield is one of those astounding souls who persevered
with a dream well beyond the point when most of us would have
given up. His example challenges us to look at our own attitude
toward setbacks, and whether we let them deter us too easily from
reaching our goals.

The setbacks we suffer in pursuing dreams and goals range from
minor ones to major defeats and losses. Whether we realize it or
not, we each are predisposed to interpret setbacks in a particular
way; we have a bias toward what they mean for us. For most people,
the default interpretation is pessimistic. They may regard a small

number of setbacks as an ominous sign that God disapproves of their dream. Even a single defeat may discourage them from trying again.

Others, like Canfield, are slow to regard any disappointment as signaling that their dream is unworthy. A publisher's rejection—the end of the journey for many aspiring writers—for Canfield was merely a speed bump in the road of life.

If we're to realize the potential God has given us, and discover his best for us in any area, it's critical that we develop an optimistic bias toward setbacks. I'm not suggesting we become bullheaded and never assume God is signaling his disapproval of our plans. Every defeat we experience is unique, and each deserves some scrutiny. On occasion, God will use a setback to show that a dream isn't right for us, or that we should change our approach in some way.

Yet often we simply have no way of immediately knowing the significance of a setback, if there is any. If we've had good reason to believe a dream is valid in the first place, then we ought to regard any deterrent as temporary—and even assume it may have hidden benefit. This optimistic bias is vital for several reasons:

• For one thing, we humans are loss-averse, as we noted earlier. We detest losing. Countless studies have shown that we attach greater value to losses than to successes of equal value. The pain we suffer in losing $1,000 is greater than our joy in gaining $1,000, for instance.

Consider the anguish of the shepherd in Jesus' parable over losing just one sheep from his fold, even though 99 remained (Lk 15: 4-7). Or the distress of the woman who lost one gold coin, even though she still had nine (Lk 15:8-10).

One result of loss aversion is that setbacks can discourage us so profoundly that we lose the heart to try again, even when our prospects for success continue to be good. Severe losses can shell shock us. Psychologist Martin Seligman and colleagues describe the problem as "learned helplessness."[1] Several failures may numb us into thinking we simply can't succeed at a certain endeavor, and we feel powerless to break the inertia of defeat.

While some disappointment in the face of defeat is normal, an optimistic outlook protects us from caving in to excessive discouragement that immobilizes us.

• On the positive side, an optimistic perspective toward setbacks energizes us, fuels our creativity, and helps us recognize new alternatives for reaching our dream.

• An optimistic outlook also honors God. Scripture stresses that God, far from being capricious, loves us infinitely and desires the very best for us. He is endlessly creative in providing for us. He often takes what to us appears to be a circuitous route in moving us to a new horizon.

Prevailing pessimism about setbacks always means we're assuming God has less than our best interests in mind. Optimism helps us to think more clearly about God's broader intentions, and to recognize creative alternatives he may be presenting. It enables us to reverence and love him, and opens us more fully to his guidance.

Optimism, in short, helps us to love God in the far-reaching manner Jesus spoke of when he said, "Love the Lord your God with all your heart and with all your soul and with all your strength and with all your mind" (Lk 10:27).

Learning Optimism

How, then, do we gain such an outlook? It helps us to clearly understand the different ways we can perceive a personal loss. There are actually nine possibilities. Recognizing them, and understanding their dynamics, helps us to pinpoint what our own reaction to hurdles typically is. It also broadens our awareness of optimistic options, giving us greater potential for viewing a difficult situation positively.

Ranging from most pessimistic to most optimistic, we might perceive a setback as:

1. God's punishment for our sin
2. God's indication that he disapproves of our succeeding

3. The result of our own failure, destroying our chance of ever succeeding

4. The result of our own failure, but providing a beneficial lesson that will help us succeed

5. A random occurrence

6. God's "closing a door to open a window"

7. A "teaser" from life, when in fact we're on the brink of succeeding

8. A gateway to success; if we respond to this defeat properly, it will help us reach our goal

9. A success that merely appears to be a setback.

Yes, *whew!*

The most encouraging part about making this list is to note how many positive options there are for interpreting setbacks. Six of the possibilities are optimistic—ranging from moderately to outlandishly so. In spite of this, many people regard most defeats they suffer as one of the first three purely pessimistic options. Not a few interpret all setbacks as options 1 or 2: God is either punishing them or showing his disapproval of their effort—or both.

Yet Scripture couldn't be clearer that God is vastly more creative and loving than this in directing our lives. We find so many examples of options 4-9 as we observe his role in people's lives in the Bible, that these should slant our assumptions about setbacks optimistically.

Worst-Case Scenarios (Options 1 and 2)

This isn't to say we should close our eyes to the possibility God might be chastening us through a setback. Yet if this is the case, then we may assume he will make it unmistakably clear. At the very least, the connection between the sin we've committed and the event indicating God's judgment will be obvious. The man imprisoned for forgery may rightly assume God is punishing him through his incarceration.

Yet I'm stretching things to think that my computer crashing today is God's punishment for lustful thoughts I fantasized yesterday. So often the cause-effect associations we make in assuming God's judgment are every bit this hazy. When the connection is this vague, we may rest assured God isn't chastening us through the unwelcome event, and open ourselves to more optimistic possibilities.

We should feel even greater freedom to dismiss any thought that God is showing through a setback that he doesn't want us to succeed. While it's possible he's indicating a specific goal isn't right for us (more on that in a moment), he is, emphatically, not demonstrating that he's against our succeeding in general.

Many Christians assume that God doesn't want them to enjoy significant success. To succeed in reaching some cherished goal would make them more like God, more competitive with God, too subject to pride.

Yet Scripture teaches that God has made us *in his image.* It first presents this astonishing insight in Genesis 1:26-27, immediately following the account of God's creating the universe, the inhabited world and humankind. In the same breath, it tells us that God commanded people to take control of creation, to "subdue the earth," to bring order to life in beneficial ways (Gen 1:26-30, 2:19-20). To be in God's image, then—and to live reverently in light of it—is to be creative and productive. We glorify God by setting ambitious goals and living productively! Where we err is in not seeking his guidance about the goals we set, and in not praising him for what we're able to accomplish. But we're cooperating with God, not fighting him, by making a reasonable effort to succeed.

Whatever else we conclude about a setback, we may take heart that it's not showing God is against our being successful.

Worst-Case Scenarios (Option 3)

Even if we conclude God isn't expressing his judgment against us through a setback, we may still be too hard on ourselves about what happened. Indeed, the unwelcome outcome may be our fault entirely. Yet we need to be patient and forgiving, not only with others, but with ourselves. We'll make many mistakes as we pursue any goal, and God graciously gives us many second chances.

Our most tragic assumption is that some mistake we've made is the *ultimate* failure, a foul-up forever condemning us to a less meaningful life. "I'm washed up," we may be tempted to say.

The most effective antidote against losing heart is to develop an earnest desire to learn and grow through our mistakes. They provide the best possible means for learning firsthand how not to do something, and thus how to be more successful in the future.

I learned this lesson in eighth grade—of course, the hard way. A band I had formed, "The Galaxies," was scheduled to perform for an in-school talent assembly. We fully expected to give a top performance and be counted as class heroes for the rest of the year.

We walked on stage to tremendous applause, our heads swelling with pride. But shortly after we began playing, my guitar amp went silent. The wires connecting the guitar cord to the amp's input jack had pulled loose. An electric guitar without amplification is about as useful as a TV not turned on, and since I was the only lead player, we had no choice but to stop the song. I bent down and, for several anxious minutes, struggled to reattach the wires to the jack, but in my franticness only snapped them off the cord. As I fumbled, the students grew noisy. Finally, the principal stepped up to the microphone. He proceeded to chastise the students for being rowdy, and ordered them back to class.

Far from being heroes, our classmates looked on us as stooges who kept them from having a good time. The shame and humiliation we felt was immense.

In time, however, I came to count this experience as one of the most beneficial of my life. Through it I discovered unforgettably the need for preparation. When a guitar cord would break again at a future performance, there was an extra handy to replace it. The event touched my life broadly, and drove me to go the extra mile in preparing for everything I do. No textbook or lecture could have taught me the lesson nearly as well.

Regardless of our age or position in life, every mistake we make has the potential to teach us critical lessons. To think any has no such benefits is wrong. We should strike option 3 from our list, and consider every failure, at the least, as option 4.

Even the most devastating personal failure—one that impairs our health, for instance—still gives us a basis for teaching others how to avoid the same pitfall. Most of our mistakes, of course, aren't nearly so catastrophic. Being eager to learn from them, and to help others through their lessons, will protect us from caving in to regret. It will help us find the heart to leave the past behind and move on.

Best-Case Scenarios

In so many cases, we simply can't relate a setback clearly to God's judgment or to some mistake of ours. And we have no immediate way of knowing why God allowed it to happen, and may never know. What's thrilling on these occasions is that we're left conscience-free to entertain the most optimistic possibilities. Often, too, we have considerable freedom to affect the consequences—even to convert a defeat into a success.

Even if the setback does stem from our failure or God's judgment, it's still possible that God, who is infinitely creative with us, will use it in one of the positive ways we've mentioned.

We should develop the habit, with every significant setback, of considering all the possible explanations, beginning with the most optimistic. We should let our mind function like a computer chip—scanning all the options, with a bias that one of the most optimistic explains it. If we can't quickly determine this is so, we should cherish hope that it will prove to be in time.

We ought to strive also to understand these options thoroughly. Being keenly aware of these explanations improves the chance we'll respond a setback in the most positive possible spirit.

Let's look briefly at some dynamics of options 4-9. We'll start at the top of the list and work down, since this is how we should scan the possibilities when we need to.

• *A success that we've misperceived as a setback.* We should always begin by considering carefully whether a "setback" is really so. In a discouraged spirit, we can easily miss certain details that give a different interpretation.

In *Faith and Optimism* I describe an occasion when I misread an insurance invoice, thinking it was a bill for $1,500. In fact, I missed the letters "CR" following the dollar amount. The misperception was significant, for I had petitioned the company to reduce our ministry's quarterly payment and to reimburse us past overpayments. I thought the invoice indicated I'd failed, when it fact it showed I'd succeeded!

With every apparent setback we ought first to take a deep breath, and then look closer at the details. Am I really perceiving this situation correctly? Sometimes we're pleasantly surprised by what a more careful look reveals.

• *A gateway to success.* In a similar way, many situations we initially perceive as defeats actually offer us special opportunities to move toward our goal. If we're alert to this, we can turn such setbacks into successes.

I learned this lesson some years ago when Evie and I placed our former home on sale. Our agent advised us that visitors who merely made nice comments would probably not end up making us an offer. The one who buys it would first seem dissatisfied and ask some hard questions.

His prediction proved prophetic. Four or five friendly people visited, praising the house, but afterwards not showing further interest. Then a stern-faced man walked through, criticizing small imperfections and asking questions the others hadn't raised. The next day he tendered an offer, for exactly the price we were willing to accept.

His behavior demonstrates a principle every good salesperson understands well. A customer's initial negative reaction doesn't necessarily mean no sale. It may indicate she's warming to the purchase, but working through the issues and emotions involved (Prov 20:14). By patiently addressing her concerns, she may be won over.

The more general lesson for each of us is that someone's negative response to us on any matter isn't necessarily their final word. It may actually indicate they're open to our further input. "Through patience a ruler can be persuaded, and a gentle tongue can break a bone" (Prov 25:15).

Situations we perceive as setbacks may help us move toward our goals in other ways. Here we should keep in mind a fascinating principle of physics—that it's possible to sail against the wind. The same wind that pushes a boat backward can draw it forward, if the sail is fashioned and tilted correctly. In the same way, a circumstance with the potential to push us away from a goal may also allow us to move toward it, if we respond properly. We should always be alert to opportunities life offers us to sail against the wind.

• *A teaser from life, when in fact we're on the brink of succeeding.* The notion that setbacks are often a prelude to success is a favorite theme of motivational writers, who may overdo the point. Yet consider the observation of human potential researcher Napoleon Hill, in one of the twentieth century's most popular self-help books: "More than five hundred of the most successful men this country has ever known told the author their greatest success came just one step *beyond* the point at which defeat had overtaken them. Failure is a trickster with a keen sense of irony and cunning. It takes great delight in tripping one when success is almost within reach."[2]

Hill's claim is intriguing, for most of us, I suspect, at least occasionally have had parallel experiences. We've earnestly pursued a goal, only to suffer a crippling setback we feared spelled the end of our dream. Yet a short time later, we enjoyed an unexpected breakthrough, which allowed us to succeed. Hill's reflection brings to mind that Satan is alive and well, and will do anything possible to divert us from ends God wants us to achieve. It's well within his nature to bring defeat across our path just as we're on the verge of victory.

The other side of this factor is that God uses certain unwelcome events to test and prepare us to handle success. One reason he works this way is to build into us healthy humility. He does so also to strengthen our faith and our ability to stay hopeful in the face of discouragement.

If we don't have clear evidence a setback is God's signal to abandon a dream, then the possibility remains it's a teaser—either a diversion from Satan, or a growth experience from God. It's good for us to stay hopeful this proves true. In that spirit, we'll be alert to opportunities God provides to regain our footing.

• *God's closing a door to open a window.* With hindsight, we often realize God was gracious to terminate certain situations we now recognize weren't good for us. In other cases, we realize he brought something good to a close in order to bring something better into our life. Most happily married people I know will admit they're now grateful to God that certain past relationships failed. As painful as the breakups were, they cleared the way for him to bring someone more suitable across their path.

In still other cases, we may wince at thinking it was God who brought about a difficult loss. Still, we now realize he has supplied stunningly for the void it left. A friend who endured an excruciating marriage breakup a year ago, recently told me he's now filled with eager anticipation to see how God will provide for him.

My friend's attitude is what ours ideally should be once we've properly grieved a major loss. We should eagerly expect that God will "open a window" to compensate for the door that's been shut.

This isn't to underestimate the challenge of determining if a door is truly closed. How can we recognize when a defeat is final, and when we should keep trying?

Here—to review the principle we discussed in chapter 4—the critical question is how broad a goal or dream is. We should be slow ever to think God has permanently closed the door on long-term dreams based on how he has gifted and motivated us. But certain narrower goals we set toward achieving these dreams are a different matter. If we've tried reasonably to reach a certain one without success, we should conclude that door is shut and try a different alternative.

Again, to cite the marriage example: If the evidence suggests God has created me to be married, I should hold fast to the dream of finding someone for as long as it takes. But I shouldn't hold on indefinitely to the hope of marrying someone who fails to show interest. After making a reasonable effort to win that person's affection, I need to accept that this specific door is shut, and look for someone else.

The Book of Ruth is one of Scripture's most inspiring pictures of God's providing for people after devastating losses. Ruth and Naomi, both bereft of their husbands, find new outlets for their affection—Ruth in a new marriage, and Naomi in a grandchild born to Ruth. The Book of Ruth shows that it's God's nature to provide new beginnings when we've suffered defeat. Like my friend who suffered the broken marriage, we have every reason to expect special help from God at such a time.

• *A random occurrence.* In his *Learned Optimism*, Martin Seligman stresses that a vital step toward optimism is learning to recognize when setbacks are merely random occurrences.[2] We may panic at an unwelcome event, assuming it signals the bottom is falling out everywhere else in our life. In reality, the fact a stock I own drops drastically this morning doesn't mean my boss is going to fire me this afternoon, or that my girlfriend will break up with me this evening. The points in our lives where we fear calamity so often are largely unrelated.

While it may be argued no event is truly random in God's sight, it's right to regard many as such from our human standpoint. When we assume connections that aren't naturally there, we obsess unreasonably about the broader implications of just one defeat. And by brooding so globally about our life, we're imagining God as our enemy, not our friend. We're assuming he's showing through this one setback that he'll work against in other ways also.

Yet defeat in one area may just as well indicate we're in store for a victory in another as anything. Regarding setbacks as random allows us to turn the tables on catastrophizing, and instead to imagine that success may be around the corner. When this perspective is added to the others we're considering, we have a profoundly optimistic basis for expecting the best from God when life deals us a curve ball.

* * * * * * * *

I realize this chapter's perspective is somewhat complicated, and presents a lot to hold in your mind at once. Yet the effort is worth it, I assure you, especially if you're one who tends to obsess too much over obstacles, or to give up too quickly on your goals. If either of these are your tendencies, I urge you to reread this chapter several times; memorize the eight options for judging setbacks, and internalize this list as best as you can. Then, when setbacks occur, make it a habit to scan the options, and to apply the most reasonably optimistic to your predicament. This practice can revolutionize the way you respond to defeats and challenges, and help greatly to keep you on course toward your dreams.

IV

Reaping the Harvest

16

Joyfully Succeeding

I can learn to counteract any tendency to sabotage my dreams, and be ready both to succeed and to enjoy my victories.

A GREAT AUNT OF MINE, after finishing high school, enrolled in college. She faithfully pursued her academic program for nearly four years. Then, two weeks before graduation—she quit. Although only a few assignments remained, she claimed she'd lost interest and saw no purpose in completing the degree.

My aunt's stunning decision demonstrates one of human nature's greatest ironies. Even when a goal is achievable for us, we may still bail out, or do something so counterproductive that it prevents our success. Our uneasiness with succeeding can lead us to sabotage dreams that are well within our reach.

As dearly as we may long for success on one level, we may dread it on another. If our wariness doesn't spur us to do something insidious to thwart our achievement, it may still prevent us from truly enjoying it, or from fully reaping its benefits.

My aunt's behavior was extreme, unquestionably. The actions

we may take to derail a dream, or to dampen our joy in succeeding, are often more subtle and ingenious. They're often so subconsciously driven that we fail to recognize we've sabotaged our goal. Have you ever caught a cold just before giving a talk or vocal performance? Suffered an accident en route to a job interview or important meeting? Had a falling out over something minor with someone in a position to help you? Such incidents can indicate you're uneasy with success.

I say *can,* for the fact we suffer a setback doesn't necessarily mean we fear succeeding or are being restrained subconsciously. Yet our fear of success can induce our subconscious to act against us.

We spoke earlier of the importance of managing our own temperament, if we're going to achieve a dream. I looked at the need to understand our potential for despair, which can set in if we're convinced the odds are too stacked against us. If we recognize what triggers this overblown fear of failure, we'll be less susceptible to its shutting us down, and better able to take it in stride and stay focused. Yet it's just as important to understand our potential to fear *success*, and be ready to tame our anxieties about succeeding. This is also a vital part of managing our temperament, and it deserves our careful attention now.

Why We Fear Success
1. The fear of losing others' approval. I don't know what prompted my aunt, long deceased, to opt out of college so close to finishing. I do have a strong suspicion. It was unusual enough for a woman to attend college in the early 1900s, let alone graduate. She may have feared others would think her too driven by masculine instincts if she gained the degree. Marriage suitors might be frightened away.

If I'm right, then she demonstrates one of the most common reasons we dread success: we fear offending others whose affection we prize.

While the social climate has improved radically for woman in the century since my aunt abandoned college, many still worry that success will hinder their romantic aspirations. Will that promotion or advanced degree work against me in relationships? Will it alienate the man who wants to feel superior, or who's looking for a woman more drawn to domestic life?

Both men and women worry about the impact of success on friendships and family relationships. Will those who love me as I am now still like me as much if I succeed? Will they think I've acted pridefully by pursuing my dream? Will they be offended or withdraw their affection—even in subtle ways?

If such concerns grow strong enough, we may let a dream go, even though our prospects for success are good.

2. The fear of one-upping others. We may also feel uneasy about succeeding in an area where a family member or close friend has failed. Our success might cause them to feel the pain of their failure even more greatly, we imagine, and so we fear hurting them. Even if this person is rooting for us to succeed, we may still feel it's inappropriate to allow ourselves to enjoy a benefit they failed to attain.

In her mammoth fifteen-year study of the effects of divorce on children, Judith Wallerstein observes that women whose mothers suffered a failed marriage often feel guilty availing themselves of a good opportunity to marry. It isn't fair to let themselves enjoy bliss that mom didn't.[1]

Men may also hold back from marriage out of a similar concern of hurting their father. More typically, though, they fear one-upping him professionally, and may feel guilty excelling in a career where he failed.

3. Breaking the comfort zone of failure. A more subtle problem occurs if we experienced failure while growing up, to the point we became accustomed to not succeeding. Failure may now be such a familiar experience that we feel uncomfortable breaking its inertia.

The challenge can be especially great if we were *rewarded* for failing. A child may find his problems bring him more welcome attention than his achievements. Take Sarah, a fifth grader, whose parents have an unstable marriage. Her folks are so preoccupied with their own problems that, when she brings home good marks, they scarcely notice. Yet when the principal phones to tell them Sarah skipped school, they stop fighting long enough to focus on helping her work through her problems. Sarah not only cherishes the attention, but relishes the fact that her misbehavior has encouraged at least temporary harmony between her parents.

If a child has enough experiences like this, she may grow to regard failure as rewarding. "If I succeed, who notices?" she thinks; "if I fail, I'm consoled." As an adult, she may strongly want to succeed in certain areas, yet be held back by the force of these expectations established in childhood, which are now largely subconscious.

4. The fear of punishment from God. The most crippling anxiety some people suffer about success is that God will punish them if they reach their goal. God knows they don't deserve to succeed, they assume. He won't like it if they do. He will crown their victory with misfortune.

The fear of God's punishment for succeeding is a natural human instinct, and more deeply imbedded than many realize. So much so, that many primitive religions have rituals for appeasing the gods upon achieving personal success.

In *Overcoming the Fear of Success*, therapist Martha Freedman tells of a carpenter she counseled who, fulfilling a life's dream, worked diligently at building a first-class racing boat. Yet he couldn't bring himself to apply the final coat of paint, fearing once he completed his project, he'd die. The story does have a happy ending. With Freedman's help, he found the courage to take that step. He didn't die or suffer disaster. To the contrary, he found succeeding so exhilarating that it inspired him to launch a career building master racing craft. Yet his example shows how insidiously the fear of God's punishment can blunt our creative output.[2]

It's not unusual for Christians, who believe strongly in the grace and forgiveness of God, and in his rewards for obedience, to also fear his displeasure over achieving personal dreams. We're inconsistent creatures, and may even believe that God is calling us to pursue a goal and, at the same time, fear his chastisement if we succeed.

5. The "Impostor Phenomenon." We may be troubled as well by the fear we're incompetent or unfit for a new responsibility. Since we believe we're misrepresenting ourselves to others, we worry that God will sabotage our success, or that we're destined to do something embarrassing to trip ourselves up.

In *If I'm So Successful, Why Do I Feel Like a Fake?*, Joan Harvey documents how many highly-skilled professionals, who receive well-deserved promotions, still obsess about being unqualified for their new positions—a problem she terms the Impostor Phenomenon. Not a few fear that some mortifying incident will derail their career, exposing them to the world as a fake. It's common for those with impostor fears to ruminate that "the Big One is coming."[3]

Fears of incompetence may plague us in areas besides career, including ministry and social service work, parenting, and building relationships.

Part of the problem, Harvey explains, is that taking on new responsibility requires us to assume new roles. It's normal to feel uncomfortable with these untrodden identities at first, since we're unfamiliar with them. We may interpret this uneasiness as signaling we're being inauthentic fulfilling these roles—unfaithful to our true inner self. We may worry, too, that others view us as insincere.

Impostor fears can prompt us to opt out of positions for which we're, in fact, well-qualified. They may also discourage us from pursuing opportunities that fit us well.

6. An excessive concern with owning our own life. Another reason we may resist success illustrates one of the most debilitating ways our psyche can function. We may feel uneasy achieving a goal because we know others *want* us to succeed. Our need for control is so great that we want to avoid any semblance of living out others' expectations—even *positive* ones. We don't want to give anyone the gratification of rejoicing in our success, or of thinking they helped us by cheering us on.

It's not unusual, for instance, for a grown son or daughter to choose a career different from the one their parents wish, even if he or she would otherwise prefer that option.

When our concern with owning our life is healthy, we naturally wish to act against others' negative expectations. When we feel compelled to defy their *positive* expectations, we've taken the need to own our life to an unfortunate level. At this point, we may feel uneasy succeeding in any way at all, for it's difficult to find any worthy goal that at least some people aren't rooting for us to achieve.

7. Fear of increased responsibility and losing freedom. There's also a reason we can fear success that isn't complicated or difficult to understand at all. We worry that the increased responsibilities of reaching a goal will be too burdensome. While this fear is sometimes justified, it often amounts to focusing too greatly on the challenges of achieving a dream, rather than the benefits.

Success typically reduces our freedom in certain ways, and that concern can also be unsettling. We don't like having our options reduced in any way, and we exhilarate in being as broadly free to choose as possible. The fear of losing freedom is the most common reason people who dearly want to be married still opt out of good opportunities. It's also why many fail to pursue golden prospects in career and other areas.

Turning the Tide

While there are other reasons we may fear success, these are some of the major ones. They're enough to show that we're complex creatures psychologically, and may desire success greatly on one level, yet resist it on another. Even if we aren't susceptible at most of these points, we may still be at one or more, to the point that we sabotage good opportunities or fail to benefit fully from our victories.

The good news is that we can fight back. We can change self-defeating patterns, and even reverse tendencies that thwart our dreams.

If you're uncomfortable with success, can you clarify why? Consider the possible reasons I've suggested, and see if any of these shoes fit. Can you identify certain outlooks that diminish your zeal to succeed? Write them down. Be as specific as you can.

Perhaps you avoid success for reasons you *can't* clearly specify. You only know that you fall in to the same self-defeating behavior time and again, but don't understand why. If so, then I urge you to seek a professional counselor's help. You're dealing with a formidable problem that you're unlikely to conquer on your own. With a counselor's direction, you can identify factors that have programmed you instinctively to court failure rather than success. Most important, you can determine steps that will change the pattern, and allow you to begin following your dreams more effectively.

Paradigm Shifts Regarding Success

You may be only too aware of why you fear success. You clearly recognize that certain assumptions you hold are the problem. You may not need professional counseling to untangle deep-seated complexes. But you do need to develop more healthy thinking about success, and to revise patterns of thinking that are working against you. Here are some outlooks that can help.

• *God's will and my success.* The belief that God may punish us for succeeding usually springs from humility that, in itself, is commendable. As Christians, we're only too aware that our motives, even in pursuing the noblest goal, are mixed at best. As we grow in Christ, we become more conscious of unhealthy motives— a function of coming closer to his light and being exposed by it. And recognizing that our motives are less than perfect may lead us to fear God's retribution if we succeed.

Scripture also stresses that we shouldn't cherish grandiose ideas about ourselves (Rom 12:3, Phil 2:3), and warns us constantly to be on guard against any attraction becoming an idol.

Yet failure, in its own strange way, can become an idol to us—every bit as greatly as success. And our motives in courting failure can be just as unhealthy as in chasing some totally selfish goal.

In pursuing any dream, we should strive to keep our relationship with Christ strong, and pray earnestly that God will give us motives honoring to Christ. Yet, as Paul reminds us graphically in Romans 7, we can never rid ourselves fully of selfish intentions this side of eternity. If we let ourselves be obsessed with motives, we'll become convinced we're unworthy of any accomplishment, and be immobilized.

Our life is of far greater benefit to others—and to Christ's mission—when we focus our energy primarily, not upon motives, but upon realizing our best potential for Christ. Consider that Paul, in his extensive teaching on spiritual gifts, never tells believers to refrain from using their gifts because of imperfect motives. He consistently counsels us to diligently employ our gifts for the benefit of others. He surely recognized that our motives would sometimes be less than ideal in this process.

Scripture not only teaches that God gives us potential and golden opportunities, but that he wants us to *rejoice* in our successes. The Israelites were instructed to set aside a tithe of their produce to eat before the Lord in a spirit of celebration (Deut 12:5-19; 14:22-27). They were *commanded* to rejoice over what God had enabled them to accomplish! The stunning implication is that God takes joy in our accomplishments and wishes to rejoice with us in our victories.

God desires not that we deny our personal dreams, but that we pursue them *in companionship with him.* He wants us to pursue a dream as an odyssey traveled with him—an adventure where we seek his guidance, strength and provision, then rejoice with him in our successes. When we imagine God being against our succeeding, we're thinking of him as our adversary rather than our friend. Nothing helps more to combat our fears of success than to appreciate God as our companion who is cheering us on as we move toward our goals.

• *Will others be hurt by my succeeding?* In developing a healthy outlook on success, we also need to come to terms with concerns about others' reactions. The perception that others don't want us to succeed sometimes has basis. But remember that God has made human nature remarkably resilient. We can bear the disappointment of lost affection if something positive takes its place. It can be a worthwhile tradeoff to let go of some affirmation in order to experience the joy of using our gifts more fully. And as we take steps of growth, we best position ourselves to develop new friendships. In the long run, we're happier in relationships with those who desire God's best for us than with those who insist we conform to their still-life pictures.

But what about the fear that our success will dishearten our parents or others who are discouraged about their own failures? The concern not to hurt others by outshining them can spring from compassion, respect, and a genuine desire to promote their welfare. Still, it's always a case of assuming responsibility that isn't properly ours, and indicates we've been drawn in to a codependent mentality. Following Christ means learning not only to trust our own life into his hands, but others' lives as well.

If my success causes my parents or anyone else to feel dejected, they're basing their self-worth on the wrong factors to begin with. They need to grow, rather than for me to adjust my plans to their expectations. They'll only be fulfilled when they accept God's unique plan for them, and learn to make the best of their own opportunities. Until they stop measuring their happiness against others' successes and failures, they're doomed to stay frustrated. I'm not helping them change by accommodating their unhealthy outlook, but am helping it become more deeply ingrained. I'll best serve them by refusing to let their attitude dampen my zeal. I should remember, too, that, beyond these people, many others will benefit from my success, for it will better equip me to serve their needs. I will best love them by pursuing my dream.

• *Living out others' positive expectations.* But what if my determination to own my life is so great that I'm ruffled even by the thought of fulfilling others' positive expectations? I need to begin by recognizing the sheer futility of my position. Since it's unlikely I'll accomplish any worthwhile goal without pleasing at least some people, I'm effectively blocking myself from achieving any personal dream.

I also need to redefine what it means to own my own life. Rather than think, "I'll avoid living out others' expectations at any cost," I should think, "I'm going to realize my dreams regardless of what anyone thinks. If someone is gratified by my victory, or believes their well-wishes have helped me succeed, let them think whatever they want. I won't let anyone's expectations—positive or negative—deter me from doing what's right for me."

I should pray also that God will help me keep the urge to own my life within reasonable bounds. A moderate desire to own our life serves us much better than an extreme one.

• *Dealing with impostor feelings.* We may also have to deal with feelings of fraudulence related to a dream we've achieved or wish to pursue. Here, we should remember that throughout Scripture God takes individuals and, in spite of many inadequacies, uses them in highly effective ways.

The Bible is also flooded with examples of individuals who fulfilled God's will by taking on various roles that probably didn't feel fully natural to them at first, and in some cases may never have. Moses and Jeremiah were both frightened of public speaking (Ex 4:10-13, Jer 1:6; *terrified* is probably the better word in Moses' case). Gideon suffered such low self-esteem that he was incredulous when the angel insisted he was the right man to lead Israel's army against Midian (Judg 6:15). We infer from the various times Paul exhorted Timothy not to be afraid, to rekindle his gift or to apply himself to his pastoral task, that Timothy was uneasy with his pastoral identity, and may well have suffered impostor feelings (1 Tim 4:12, 4:14-15, 5:23; 2 Tim 1:7, 1:8; cp. 1 Cor 16:10). This is in spite of the fact that Timothy is set forth as the prototype of a good pastor in the New Testament.

We may take comfort in knowing that following God's will at times *requires* we assume new roles that don't immediately feel natural, and that we live with them until they become part of our personality.

• ***Bearing the burden.*** We may also worry that success will saddle us with responsibility too burdensome for us. This fear is sometimes justified, and helps guard us against a "rescue" mentality. Yet it's often unreasonable, and may hold us back from opportunities that will truly improve our life.

How, then, can we determine if our apprehensions are reasonable? We should look honestly at what our real concern is. Am I worried that success will bring with it *too much* responsibility? Or am I more concerned about being able to handle the responsibility psychologically?

Will success so tax my time and energy, for instance, that it jeopardizes my family life or other important commitments? If so, then I need to address the problem carefully. Is it possible to delegate responsibility, so that I'm able to accomplish more with the same effort? Often the answer is yes. But if the answer is clearly no, then I shouldn't pursue my dream until I'm certain I can handle it's duties without unhealthy tradeoffs.

Often, though, our real concern is whether we can psychologically handle new responsibility that otherwise fits the limits of our time and energy fine. A job I'm offered requires public speaking, for instance, which frightens me. In this case, I should see the new opportunity as a chance to grow. I should recall past occasions when God gave me strength under fire that I thought wasn't possible for me. I should remind myself constantly that this same God will support me in my new challenges. I have a remarkable opportunity to reach new horizons—both in faith and in personal skill.

If an opportunity otherwise matches me well, and doesn't tax my time and energy unreasonably, I should see its psychological challenges as occasions to rise to, and open myself to God's new adventure. In this case, I benefit far more greatly by staring fear down than by caving in.

• *A tradeoff worth making.* What often worries us most about new responsibility isn't that it will be too burdensome or psychologically challenging, but that we'll lose freedom by taking it on. Regardless how strongly we desire the benefits an opportunity offers, committing to it means forsaking other choices. Some people dwell so much on the freedom they'll lose by achieving even a cherished dream that they conclude the tradeoff isn't worth it.

It helps to remember the problem of loss aversion, which we've spoken of several times. We humans instinctively invest greater emotion in losses than we do in gains of equal value. The sorrow we feel over losing a sum of money is greater than our pleasure over winning the same amount. Our devastation in losing a friendship is stronger than our joy in gaining a new friendship. And we can focus so greatly on what we have to give up to reach a goal, that success feels more like failure.

The best way to fight this tendency is to make a determined effort to concentrate on the benefits of accomplishing our dream. The man, for instance, who feels weak-kneed about committing to marriage, even in the face of a welcome opportunity, should focus as fully as he can upon the improvements it will bring to his life. He may find it helpful to take a personal retreat, where he dwells on these advantages, and gives God an unhindered opportunity to deepen his passion for being married.

Meditating on the benefits of taking any step of faith will help us break the pull of loss aversion, and find the courage to move toward our dream.

* * * * * * * *

Do you find it difficult to make commitments? Do you have a history of bailing out of welcome opportunities? Do you often avoid victories that are within your reach? If you instinctively tend to thwart your own good fortune, look closely at whether a fear of success, rather than of failure, is the cause. If so, then focus more on this chapter than any other in this book. Carefully consider the ways we can fear success that I've outlined, and try to identify precisely what it is about succeeding that you personally dread.

Then take the steps I've suggested for overcoming this fear, that it may no longer thwart you from reaching your goals. Commit to a dream and follow it through, no matter how much fear and trembling is involved. Make it your goal to sabotage your tendency to sabotage your dreams. The great news is that this goal is achievable! Know, especially, that God is on your side as you seek to reinvent your attitude toward success, and to realize your greatest potential for Christ.

17

Keep on Dreaming

I'll contribute most greatly to my happiness, health and effectiveness, by staying strongly committed to growing, open to new adventure, and focused on fresh dreams and goals, for as long as I'm physically and mentally able.

IN A POPULAR BOOK on realizing personal potential, entrepreneur Harvey Mackay offers a simple recipe for living successfully: You must want to achieve a dream "more than you want anything else in the world." Only pursue a goal that passionately enthralls you, Mackay insists.

But, he adds, "most important, you have to be sure you *never get it.*"[1]

Mackay is talking tongue-in-cheek, of course. He isn't recommending we prevent ourselves from reaching our dreams, nor is he encouraging self-sabotage. Nor is he saying we shouldn't celebrate our victories. Far from it. What he *is* saying is that we shouldn't let a success become our final resting place. We should take what inspiration from it we can, and then move on to new pursuits.

We do best not to let ourselves feel *too* successful, in other words. It's far healthier to continue to feel that we still have worlds to conquer. He adds, "The successful people I know always have a carrot in front of them, slightly out of reach, no matter how many carrots they already have."[2]

John Updike offered similar advice to writers in a *Time Magazine* interview that I read some years ago.[3] I've never forgotten his counsel, which has seemed like a personal admonition ever since. No one "goes bad" more frequently and thoroughly than writers, Updike noted. Authors who have a brush with success may conclude too readily that anything they write is wonderfully appealing. They stop agonizing so much over their material, and begin publishing first drafts rather than third. They lose their edge, and readers lose their interest.

Humility, Updike observed, is one of the most important essentials of good writing. We who write do best not to focus on our successes—the reviews and accolades if they come. We should focus instead on the work ahead of us, and keep that challenge substantial. And we should never imagine we've reached a plateau where we no longer need the same arduous process that has given us effective writing in the past.

Psychotherapist David Richo offers such counsel more broadly in *Unexpected Miracles*. Life presents us with many welcome surprises, Richo explains. Yet we must stay adequately challenged to be poised to experience them; if we let ourselves grow too comfortable, we blunt the possibility of surprise. "Are you setting up your life so that there will be no surprises?" Richo asks. "Is everything too orderly? What do you lose that way? Is fear behind your not being surprised very much these days?"[4]

Keeping Motivation Strong

One of the greatest challenges we face is knowing how to move forward once we experience success or have a taste of it. Success can be a tonic—in the healthiest sense—boosting our self-esteem, giving us confidence we can achieve our goals, and spurring us on to new pursuits.

Success can also be a tranquilizer, lulling us in to a life that's too comfortable and predictable. Or it may inspire us to keep some challenge present, but not at a level appropriate to our potential or our need for growth and stimulation. Halford Luccock notes, "There is a major disaster when a person allows some success to become a stopping place rather than a way station on to a larger goal. It often happens that an early success is a greater moral hazard than an early failure."[5]

We're always happiest, healthiest and most productive when our life is strongly in a growth mode. We're most likely realizing our potential when we're being driven by childlike enthusiasm for a dream, which fires us to spring out of bed when the alarm rings, and move as quickly as we can to salvage every moment possible for working toward our goal.

This isn't to say that we have to have a radically new dream on the horizon at all times. Dreams that are right for us come in two varieties—those we pursue, and those we live out. Some achieve a dream early in life that fits them so well they spend the rest of their life living it out—yet they do so with energy and creative initiative. In reality, they're responding to many new dreams, but these fit clearly within the cherished role in life they've attained.

Many of us go through periods like this. We've achieved a dream so meaningful, and demanding in its responsibilities, that we're compelled to give our full attention to living it out. While we may pursue many goals related to this dream, we're wisest not to let unrelated interests divert us.

Over a lifetime, though, most of us aren't so unilateral in our approach to life, but discover God's plan through a more circuitous route. From time to time, we need a clearly new dream to keep our life on the growing edge. For us, the temptation may be to settle prematurely for a level of accomplishment that doesn't represent God's best for us.

Pacing Ourselves
In stressing the importance of continuing to grow and pursue dreams,

I don't mean to downplay our need for leisure. We each need times when we turn off the mental generator. We need rest and relaxation daily and sometimes extended periods of leisure. I've long been impressed that Scripture—especially in its Sabbath teaching—gives more emphasis to the importance of rest than work. The Bible unquestionably views overwork as a greater threat to our well-being than laziness.

Scripture extols leisure, not as an end in itself, but as a chance to rekindle our motivation for the work God has called us to do. After Ezra and his highly motivated companions traveled from the Ahava Canal to Jerusalem, for instance, they "rested three days" before proceeding with their challenging mission (Ezra 8:32). The revitalizing role of rest is shown especially dramatically in Elijah's recovery from burnout, detailed in 1 Kings 19:1-8.

Is it wrong, then, to seek leisure for its own sake? Is it unhealthy, for example, to dream of retirement as an opportunity for unending leisure?

I've personally known many retired people who for years yearned for the time when they could finally stop punching the clock and be free to enjoy life with few restrictions. Some disdained their professional work, and long endured an unsatisfying career, with the hope for a major payback in retirement. Some of them truly enjoy their retirement—and I must confess they are an inspiration to me. Their examples encourage me to take life at a more reasonable pace and not to be so obsessive about work.

When I look at *why* these people enjoy retirement so much, though, I find in every case that their life still includes plenty of activity. Some are active in recreational, artistic or creative pursuits. Others, with large extended families, are circuit riders, visiting children and grandchildren, giving encouragement and helping with problems where they can. Others give extensive time to volunteer service or ministry. Retirement for these people is a treasured opportunity to pursue dreams that have been dormant or half-realized for much of their life. They are still very much about the business of realizing their potential.

Others are bored in retirement, and some simply miserable. They had looked to retirement and its leisure as life's ultimate prize, but it hasn't delivered what it promised. They long for greater purpose in life, and a greater sense of being useful.

Others begin retirement eager to pursue certain activities that over time lose their appeal. Now they long for greater stimulation.

The challenge for those who find retirement unsatisfying is the lure of the comfort zone. Their lifestyle now at least is comfortable and familiar. And they no longer have financial pressure—a greater benefit than we usually realize—to look for employment. The inertia can be broken in such cases. But it takes courage and decisiveness. It may also require defying conventional wisdom.

Retirement as Sabbatical?
One such individual who defied both inertia and conventional wisdom, and long benefited, was Robert Eisenberg. After working half a century in garment manufacturing, Eisenberg retired in 1970 at 72, selling Zabin Industries, which he had owned since 1954. "I was ready [for retirement]," he said, "but I found it boring after about 10 years." At 82, he went back to work for Zabin, and continued working full-time for the company until 104, overseeing zipper production. "He's got remarkable mental abilities," owner Alan Failoa commented when Eisenberg was 103. "The longer I've dealt with him, the more I find myself forgetting his age."[6]

It may be argued that his was simply a case of exceptional genetics. Yet it's hard to resist the conclusion that Eisenberg's decision to resume his former career added years to his life; it certainly added vitality to his years. His example is unusual (he was believed by many then to be America's oldest worker), and I'm not suggesting that most who are bored in retirement should jump back in to their former profession at full throttle. It is the right step for some, though. Many others who are restless in retirement will find relief in resuming some sort of gainful employment.

What's *most* helpful about Eisenberg's example is that it provides a different model for thinking about retirement than our customary one—namely, *retirement as sabbatical.* This is a much more inspiring and helpful model for many of us than the traditional concept of retirement as endless leisure, for it encourages us to realize that, if we're unhappy retired, we're not locked in to staying so. There may be a multitude of new directions we can take with our life, including many we've never entertained. These options may include resuming a meaningful career.

If you find yourself unsatisfied in retirement, at least consider the possibility that God is intending this period as a sabbatical for you rather than a permanent vacation. If you take on a job or some meaningful new activity at this point, you'll have a lifetime of experience to bring to your new calling, plus the benefit of the time you've taken to get refreshed and gain new perspective. The retirement-as-sabbatical model can be positively thrilling, especially if you've felt "put out to pasture" and doomed to stay there forever.

Embracing New Dreams

Let's say you're at a point in life where you're fairly comfortable. You may be retired. Or you may be young and working 80 hours a week. But you've achieved some goals that are important to you. Now you're content with your life as it is, and not greatly preoccupied with reaching for new horizons.

How do you determine if this comfort zone is healthy, or whether there is yet another star to which you should hitch a wagon?

One critical question is whether you're truly happy in this state. Your instincts will tell you a lot, if you read them correctly. In sorting them through, consider these questions:

• *Is there, in fact, a major improvement you would welcome for your life? Do you fantasize about having this benefit?*

• *Is there a skill you've long cherished for yourself, but have never developed or nurtured as fully as you'd like?*

• *Is there a need among people you know, or a more wide-*

spread need in the world, that you would love to help meet? Is there a problem others face that you dream of solving, or a contribution to others' lives you dream of making?

• *Suppose you were at the end of your life, looking back over it. Would you feel there is unfinished business? Is there something you would seriously regret not having accomplished?*

Perhaps it's only too clear that the answer to one or more of these questions is yes. You have a dream—dormant though it may be—that could easily resurface with the right encouragement. If so, then I urge you to consider carefully whether you're allowing the desire for security to keep you from God's best for your life.

Healthy and Unhealthy Dreams
Again, we should keep in mind that some dreams are better left unpursued. We looked at differences between healthy and unhealthy aspirations earlier. It's easy, though, to forget these distinctions, especially as we approach retirement and may have greater resources to pursue a dream. Our need to feel important, or our compassion, may lead us to fantasize about taking on a new role, when in fact we'd have little affinity for its responsibilities.

Jason, 55, has long dreamed of becoming a pastor as a retirement vocation. One motive is noble: he would thoroughly love sharing the gospel with people and having the best possible platform for winning others to Christ. He has another motive that's more complex and less trustworthy. He attended a missions conference as a young man, where the speakers urged those attending to make ministry their career. He has been dogged with guilt ever since, fearing he may have settled for God's second best by becoming an accountant. He'd relish the opportunity to atone for his possible mistake. And he'd treasure the identity of being a pastor—a status he imagines would boost his self-worth enormously.

In reality, Jason would have little heart for the endless interacting with people needed to minister effectively—the consensus building, the handholding, the motivating—not to mention the denominational politics. He would also find the preparation process for sermons and talks burdensome.

Jason's pastoral dream, in short, is based too greatly upon the benefit he imagines would come to his self-esteem, and too little on a love for the actual work he'd have to do. Each of us lays hold to a number of dreams like this during our lifetime—where we imagine we'd savor the status of a certain role, which in reality we wouldn't enjoy living out. These are dreams that are best kept in the enjoy-the-fantasy category.

Such fantasizing isn't unhealthy, providing the roles we muse about themselves aren't harmful or unhealthy. A certain amount of such unrealistic wish dreaming, in fact, is normal, and vital to being human. It's part of the necessary process of "trying on dreams"— where we sort through all the options that appeal to us, and settle on those that truly work for us. It's simply important that we develop the discernment to distinguish between those dreams that fit us well and those that don't.

But, as we've proclaimed throughout this book, we each entertain many dreams that do make good sense for us. We would not only love the distinction of achieving the dream, but would relate well to the new responsibilities. The work and lifestyle changes the dream entails would fit our gifts and personality well.

These are dreams we should be careful not to let die as life grows more comfortable. These questions I've just suggested can help us recapture dreams for which we've lost the fire, and put them on the table again.

Giving Personal Vision a Fair Chance

Perhaps you're not certain whether to answer any of these questions yes. Before you write off the possibility that important aspirations might still be brewing inside you, consider Moses' example. God called him to spend the last third of his life in a role he found immensely satisfying, as leader of Israel's exile. He thrived on the chance to shepherd his people and make a critical difference in their destiny. His relationship with God grew extraordinarily through it all, and his health seemed to benefit as well, for at the time of his death at 120, "his eyes were not weak nor his strength gone" (Deut 34:7).

Yet Moses initially held the opportunity God was offering him in contempt—even though God had spoken to him directly, with dramatic signs, and assured him of success and of every measure of divine assistance. Moses was *certain* he didn't want the job, *convinced* he would be a failure, *positive* he would detest the work. With the possible exception of Jonah, we don't find a more stunning example in Scripture of someone resisting a call and failing to appreciate the fortuitous opportunity in front of them.

The opportunity God presented Moses, though, was ideal for him and fit his gifts and personality perfectly. Moses had grown up in Pharaoh's household, and probably understood the palace culture and communication with royalty better than any Israelite living then. He had also lived for decades with Jethro, the priest of Midian, certainly learning volumes about how to be an effective spiritual leader.

Most important, Moses had a burning, though long-repressed, instinct to fight injustice and champion better conditions for his people. In his late 30s, he killed an Egyptian whom he caught abusing an Israelite. Public resentment of his vigilantism, however, compelled Moses to flee Egypt for Midian. There he married Jethro's daughter and, for the next 40 years, tended sheep for the priest. Life in Midian was comfortable for Moses—an early retirement of sorts (Ex 2:21). Now, after four decades of peaceful shepherding, the passionate zeal of his youth had all but died out. God knew it was capable of reigniting strongly, though, with the right prodding.

Moses' example strikingly reminds us that we don't always understand our own aspirations well. Fear—of both failure and success—as well as simple inertia, can keep us from perceiving what we most want to do or would be most effective doing. We shouldn't be too quick to think we've recognized all the important horizons

God has for us. Moses' experience stirs us to look carefully at whether we're allowing security needs or unreasonable fears to shut down our ability to dream.

This isn't to say that if God leads us into a new vocation after retiring, it will necessarily require the radical acceleration of activity Moses experienced. There are other important biblical examples to consider. Abraham, for instance, took a more leisurely approach to life in his later years than Moses did. Following his father's death, Abraham "went out, not knowing whither he went" (Heb 11:8 KJV). God brought major new adventures into Abraham's life: the birth of Isaac, the experience of parenting, a military mission to rescue his cousin Lot, and remarriage after Sarah's death—to name a few. Yet these events unfolded at a more relaxed pace than circumstances did for Moses. God never laid upon Abraham the intensive leadership responsibilities required of Moses. And overall, Abraham experienced much less disruption to his life than Moses did.

If Moses gives us a model of "retirement as sabbatical," then, Abraham shows us the possibility of new dreams and adventures emerging *within* retirement. We see how widely God's plans can differ for any two people. What Moses and Abraham both teach us is the importance of staying open to new adventure and of continuing to dream big about our future. We're reminded, too, that we should never assume our life's most important chapters have all been written.

Their examples also remind us that:

• *God gives us the ability to carry out important dreams, in spite of what we may perceive as inadequacies or even severe limitations.*

• *He enlightens us to such opportunities both by inspiring new dreams, and by resurfacing old ones that have long lain dormant.*

• *The fact that we're not experiencing some burning new inspiration for our future at the moment doesn't necessarily mean we'll never enjoy fresh vision again. God's timing in this matter varies greatly for each of us.*

This last point is perhaps the most encouraging of all, for we can feel guilty or disheartened when no new dream seems to be emerging. We may berate ourselves for not thinking big enough, even though we may be trying sincerely to do so. If, in fact, we're eager to grow and enjoy new adventure, and stay open and expectant about our future, and continue to pray earnestly for God's direction and strength—then we have strong reason to expect that he will, in his time, inspire fresh dreams that bring important new purpose to our life.

* * * * * * * *

Whether you're retired or approaching it, just beginning your adult journey, or somewhere in-between, I strongly hope this book has stimulated you to embrace bigger dreams for your future. And I hope you will keep this final chapter's plea in mind as you go from here, and stay open to fresh dreams once current ones are realized. Getting too comfortable is the curse of modern life; strive for adventure more than security, and never lose your willingness to risk.

I began this book by posing a question: "what if?" What if, within the foreseeable future, you can achieve a cherished dream—what would it be? I hope you've had one in mind as you've worked through this book, that it is more crystallized now, and even in the launching stage. I urge you also to ask "what if?" constantly as you move through life. Make it your lifestyle to query yourself in this way daily, and to stay forever inquisitive of both yourself and the Lord about your future. Constantly consider whether you're fully open to God's best options, and are recognizing the paths toward your fullest potential.

Too often the "what ifs" we muse about are the problems and challenges we imagine will derail a dream. And we dwell on them so greatly that they shut us down, and our dream never initiates. Make it your lifestyle to turn the tables on such ruminating, and to focus far more on the positive "what ifs" than the negative. Doing so will strengthen your desire for a dream to the tipping point— where you're emboldened to step out in faith, even though some fears and doubts remain.

I wish you every blessing from the Lord as you move forward with your life. The time God gives us on earth is limited. Yet if offers us abundant opportunities to make positive contributions to human life and to the mission of Christ. Strive to make those contributions that best reflect the unique person God has made you to be. And, as long as he gives you the ability to dream, stay open to the new horizons he has for you.

Notes

Chapter 2: Passion and Availability
[1]Henry Jonas Magaziner, *The Golden Age of Ironwork* (Ocean Pines, Md.: Skipjack Press 2000).

Chapter 4: The Triumph of Hope
[1]George Burns, *100 Years, 100 Stories* (New York: G.P. Putnam's Sons, 1996), p. viii.
[2]Susan Levine, "Minding the Elderly: As Seniors' Numbers Grow, Geriatrics Specialists Tackle a Medical Frontier," *Washington Post,* May 30, 1999, p. A1.

Chapter 5: Contentment and Motivation
[1]W. Clement Stone, *The Success System That Never Fails* (New York: Prentice Hall, 1962).

Chapter 7: Beating the Comparison Trap
[1]*Someday We'll All Be Free,* composed and performed by Charlie Hunter, featured on his compact disc *Charlie Hunter*, Blue Note, 1999.
[2]David J. Schwartz, *The Magic of Thinking Big* (New York: Simon and Schuster, 1979).
[3]Peter G. Hanson, M.D., *The Joy of Stress* (Kansas City: Andrews, McMeel and Parker, 1985).

Chapter 8: Turning the Page
[1]Dian Vujovich, "Mind Over Money," *Fidelity Focus* Magazine, summer 1999.

[2]John A. Sarkett, "How Great Traders Go Bad," *Technical Analysis of Stocks and Commodities,* July 1999, pp. 44-48.

Chapter 9: The Joy of Late Blooming
[1]M. Scott Peck, *The Road Less Traveled: A New Psychology of Love, Traditional Values and Spiritual Growth* (Touchstone Books: 1988).

Chapter 11: Cheerleaders and Mentors
[1]M. Blaine Smith, *Overcoming Shyness: Conquering Your Social Fears* (Damascus, Md.: Silver Crest Books, 2011).
[2]M. Blaine Smith, *The Yes Anxiety: Taming the Fear of Commitment in Relationships, Career, Spiritual Life, and Daily Decisions* (Damascus, Md.: Silver Crest Books, 2011).

Chapter 13: Prayer and Your Personal Dreams
[1]John Calvin, *Institutes of the Christian Religion,* 3.20.2.
[2]Andrew Murray, *With Christ in the School of Prayer* (Old Tappan, N.J.: Revell, 1974), p. 103.

Chapter 14: Meeting the Optimism Challenge
[1]Steve Simms, *Mindrobics: How to Be Happy the Rest of Your Life* (Brentwood, Tennessee: Attitude-Lifter Enterprises, 1995).

Chapter 15: Responding to Setbacks
[1]Christopher Peterson, Steven F. Maier and Martin E. P. Seligman, *Learned Helplessness: A Theory for the Age of Personal Control* (Oxford University Press, 1995).
[2]Napoleon Hill, *Think and Grow Rich* (Hollywood, Calif.: Melvin Powers, 1960), pp. 21-22.
[3]Martin E.P. Seligman, Ph.D., *Learned Optimism: How to Change Your Mind and Your Life* (New York: Alfred A. Knopf, Inc., 1991).

Chapter 16: Joyfully Succeeding
[1]Judith Wallerstein and Sandra Blakeslee, *Second Chances: Men,*

Women, and Children a Decade after Divorce (New York: Ticknor and Fields, 1990), p. 101.

[2]Martha Friedman, *Overcoming the Fear of Success* (New York: Warmer, 1980), pp. 159-68.

[3]Joan C. Harvey with Cynthia Katz, *If I'm so Successful, Why Do I Feel Like a Fake? The Impostor Phenomenon* (New York: St. Martin's Press, 1985).

Chapter 17: Keep on Dreaming

[1]Harvey Mackay, *Beware the Naked Man Who Offers You His Shirt: Do What You Love, Love What You Do, and Deliver More Than You Promise* (New York: Fawcett Columbine, 1990), p. 72.

[2]Ibid., p. 73.

[3]"Perennial Promises Kept," Paul Grey, Peter Stoler, *Time Magazine*, October 18, 1982.

[4]David Richo, Ph.D., *Unexpected Miracles* (New York: Crossroad Publishing, 1998), p. 29.

[5]Halford Luccock, from *Christian Quotation of the Day*, April 2, 2001, a daily Internet devotional no longer active.

[6]"Time Bandit," *People Magazine*, June 4, 2001, p. 128. Eisenberg was 103 at the time and died in 2002 at 104.

About the Author

Blaine Smith, a Presbyterian pastor, spent 30 years as director of Nehemiah Ministries, Inc., a resource ministry based in the Washington, D.C. area. He retired the organization in 2009, but continues to use the name Nehemiah Ministries for free-lance work.

His career has included giving seminars and lectures, speaking at conferences, counseling, and writing. He is author of ten books, including *Knowing God's Will* (original and revised editions), *Should I Get Married?* (original and revised editions), *The Yes Anxiety*, *Overcoming Shyness, Faith and Optimism: Positive Expecation in the Christian Life* (originally *The Optimism Factor*), *One of a Kind*, *Marry a Friend*, and *Reach Beyond Your Grasp*, as well as numerous articles. These books have been published in more than thirty English language and international editions. He is also lecturer for *Guidance By The Book*, a home study course with audio cassettes produced by the Christian Broadcasting Network as part of their *Living By The Book* series.

Blaine served previously as founder/director of the Sons of Thunder, believed by many to be America's first active Christian rock band, and as assistant pastor of Memorial Presbyterian Church in St. Louis. He is an avid guitarist, and currently performs with the Newports, an oldies band active in the Washington, D.C. area.

Blaine is a graduate of Georgetown University, and also holds a Master of Divinity from Wesley Theological Seminary and a Doctor of Ministry from Fuller Theological Seminary. He and Evie live in Gaithersburg, Maryland. They've been married since 1973, and have two grown sons, Benjamin and Nathan. Their first grandchild, Jackson Olen, was born to Ben and his wife Lorinda in 2009.

Blaine also authors a twice-monthly online newsletter, *Nehemiah Notes*, featuring a practical article on the Christian faith, posted on his ministry website and available by e-mail for free. You may e-mail Blaine at mbs@nehemiahministries.com.